Breaking the Idols of Your Heart

How to Navigate the Temptations of Life

DAN B. ALLENDER
& TREMPER LONGMAN III

IVP Books

An imprint of InterVarsity Press
Downers Grove, Illinois

InterVarsity Press
P.O. Box 1400, Downers Grove, IL 60515-1426
World Wide Web: www.ivpress.com
Email: email@ivpress.com

InterVarsity Press® is the book-publishing division of InterVarsity Christian Fellowship/USA®, a movement of students and faculty active on campus at hundreds of universities, colleges and schools of nursing in the United States of America, and a member movement of the International Fellowship of Evangelical Students. For information about local and regional activities, visit intervarsity.org.

Design: Rebecca Larson
Images: Veer

ISBN 978-0-8308-3441-9

Printed in the United States of America ∞

Library of Congress Cataloging-in-Publication Data

Allender, Dan B.
  [Bold purpose]
  Breaking the idols of your heart: how to navigate the temptations
of life / Dan B. Allender, Tremper Longman III.
    p. cm.
  Includes bibliographical references.
  ISBN 978-0-8308-3441-9 (pbk.: alk. paper)
  1. Bible. O.T. Ecclesiastes—Criticism, interpretation, etc. 2.
  Christian life—Biblical teaching. I. Longman, Tremper. II. Title.
  BS1475.52.A45 2007
  223'.806—dc22

                                                                    2007011185

P 24 23 22 21 20 19 18 17 16 15 14 13 12 11 10 9 8
Y 30 29 28 27 26 25 24 23 22 21 20 19 18 17 16 15

To our oldest children,

Anna and Tremper.

You have taught us to hope against hope.

𝕯

CONTENTS

ACKNOWLEDGMENTS

Working together on a project that touches the core issues of life has prompted many discussions—some that find their way into this book and others that await a time when we are mature enough to say well the insights we have vocalized to each other. We both consider our friendship, which began when we were thirteen, is a mysterious, living testament to God's surprising goodness.

Our families are the ground of our existence and an important venue where God works in our lives and woos us to himself. None have invested their lives more richly or winsomely in our labor than our wives, Becky and Alice. We consider it an incredible gift to be linked to these unquestionably godly women who both love us and enjoy us.

We owe thanks to many people who heard our ideas for this book and gave us good guidance and suggestions, but we would especially like to thank Dan McGlinchey, who took the time to read through the whole manuscript and give us his helpful advice. We also thank Nate Taylor, a young man whose creativity promises wonderful things for his future.

Most importantly, we thank our friend and editor Cindy Bunch. Her suggestions, revisions and insights have been invaluable for the final presentation. She has made it a better book.

Finally, all gratitude goes to our God, who has not only purchased us through his Son's death, but has also honored us to be colaborers with him, spreading the message of life in Christ. We are grateful men and are honored to be invited into your life to consider with you the glory of God.

INTRODUCTION
Searching for Meaning

The alarm clattered. It was an old Timex, rounded like the sun with a gold rim around the laminated face. Each time it went off, it shook the nightstand next to Noah Adamson's bed. Its early-morning clamor awakened him to what some might view as the bright beginnings of a new day.

Not Noah. Noah loved bed. With his usual groan he reached over to the nightstand, grabbed the clock, and strangled out its last sound. For a long, tempting moment he considered burrowing back under the covers again. Then the adrenalin kicked in. Before his feet hit the floor, he was already thinking about the Pearson Furniture proposal.

He usually needed the details of his morning routine to psych him for the day—sit-ups, hot shower, cold rinse, a careful shave. Today he sped through the whole sequence with his mind already at work. He was heading downstairs in his best suit when Joan called up from the kitchen, "Honey, your eggs are ready. Do you want bacon?"

"No time." He grabbed his briefcase from his downstairs desk and slipped into the kitchen. "Give the eggs to the kids, and I'll get a burrito at work."

"It'll just take a minute." She flipped a pile of scrambled eggs onto a waiting plate and handed him a glass of orange juice. "You can be out the door before the boys even wake up."

Noah took a seat. Arguing would take more time than eating. "If this day goes the way I want, I'm going to put a huge dent in Jonathan's ability to get the final nod for all major deals."

"How so?" she asked brightly.

"Too complicated to explain." He forked in the last bite of eggs and reached for his coffee mug.

Joan got the message. Conversation was not on the morning's agenda. "Well, I wish it wasn't such a battle zone for you every day." She smoothed her sixties-style apron and stared out the window with that spacy expression that always mildly annoyed him. "Try not to be too late tonight," she said. "We're starting that new Bible study, and we agreed to bring drinks. Can we leave a little early to go by the store, or do you want me to pick up the drinks before—"

"Bible study?" Noah's face creased with irritation. "Look, I'll be wiped out if the day goes well and double-wiped if it doesn't."

"Well, we promised, and you told Jack you'd be there. You said Ecclesiastes was right up your alley because you took a class in existentialism or something in college." Joan kept her voice level, but a tightening in her shoulders told Noah she was digging in. If he wanted to keep the peace, skipping the study was not an option.

"Okay," he grunted. "We'll pick up the drinks on the way. But I'm telling you that if I am a wreck, I'm not going to go to a Bible study where I have to listen to Jack Simpson wing on about his knowledge of the Bible."

Joan turned, and the look on her face sent a stab of irritable guilt through him. He knew she looked forward to Bible study evenings. She spent most of her time caring for Timmy and Ryan and the house, and she needed the social outlet. Plus, dragging him to Bible studies was her way to exact a pound of spiritual flesh for his lack of involvement in the things of God. Noah was willing to give her that— one evening a week to keep her satisfied and off his back.

"Don't worry." He told her as he reached for his briefcase again. "If I can pull off what I'm planning today—and I promise you, I will—I'll be more than a match for Jack Simpson and Ecclesiastes."

But by the time he'd backed the car out of the garage, Noah already wished he hadn't caved in about the Bible study. An evening with Ecclesiastes—what a way to unwind after a hard day. Noah had read a few sections of the book a few years *back, and what he remembered was vaguely depressing.* Eat, drink, and be merry. Everything is meaningless. Everything is merely a chasing the wind.

So why bother? He'd always liked that little slogan, "why ask why," and now it settled into his mind with a dull ache as he steered his Audi into the familiar flow of freeway traffic. His memory of Ecclesiastes fused with irritation that it did not have a clearer and more hopeful message. Why ask why—especially with Jack Simpson in the room. Jack was a successful trial lawyer, and Noah just knew he would make Ecclesiastes into a model of order and logic, practicality and boredom. Which was worse: despair or Jack?

Maybe he could find a little time to at least read a few chapters of Ecclesiastes before going to the study. That way he'd at least have a leg to stand on when Jack started—

Brake lights up ahead signaled a sudden slowdown and short-circuited Noah's reverie. But Noah was used to city traffic; he'd already spotted a gap in the next lane. Without losing speed, he eased in behind a speeding Mustang, letting the flow of traffic push the Bible study from his mind. He had more important matters to think about, anyway—such as this morning's meeting, where he planned to make his move.

Noah was a stockbroker with the Chicago office of Brothers Consolidated, a firm that traded in "shorts." Most investors buy a stock that looks as if it will increase in market value. "Shorters" buy the rights to shares but hope that the stock is overvalued and will fall so they can purchase it well under the value it currently holds.

Noah had risen through the ranks of his peers because of his penetrating guesswork in picking stocks that were likely to fall. He did his research and investigated each company's portfolio, but his real ability was in reading people—and tracking the cultures of the companies he studied. He viewed each company like a family, getting to know each family's myths, secrets and weak spots. Each corporate family is based on the CEO's personality and vision. Noah was convinced that if he got to know the background, bias, and beliefs of the people at the helm, he could predict when the company would overextend itself and tumble into the abyss. Then the sharks could move in.

That's how Noah saw himself—as a shark. He loved to travel alone in the uncharted recesses of the Internet, gulping down everything written about a corporation and its owner. He often went back to the stories written about the CEO in high school and college to discover the points of formative failure, tragedy and loss. He was a shark who knew his territory.

Noah loved his work. He loved being a shark.

And if that meant he could never stop swimming . . . well, he was willing to pay that price.

Abundant Life in a Meaningless World

As Christians, we have given our lives to Jesus. He is the center of our lives. He is our Lord and our Savior. Nothing is more important than Jesus.

Or is he?

If asked, most Christians would automatically affirm that their relationship with Jesus is central to their lives. However, further reflection might lead to another conclusion. Ask yourself these questions:

- What do you daydream about?
- How do you think about your future?
- What occupies your thoughts?
- What do you spend most of your time doing?
- What would you like to spend most of your time doing?
- In what ways do you envy others?

How does your relationship with Jesus enter into the picture? And what is it that fuels the passion of your life? If it's not Jesus, perhaps it is work, play, sports, money, the acquisition of power, family, friends, church, ministry or something else "under the sun."

The phrase "under the sun" is a familiar one to readers of the biblical book of Ecclesiastes. The Teacher in that book explores different avenues of potential meaning of life, including the ones just mentioned. Surprisingly, he comes up empty, frustrated and angry. "Everything is meaningless" is yet another frequent refrain of that book.

You see, the book of Ecclesiastes is an idol buster.

Perhaps you are familiar with the idols that are described in books like Exodus and Isaiah. These were false gods, represented by statues, that were worshiped not only by the people in the surrounding land but, tragically, by fallen Israelites as well. They had names like Baal, Marduk, Asherah and many, many others. People put these idols in the center of their life; to borrow a phrase from a mid-twentieth-century theologian, they became the people's "ultimate concern." Men and women offered them material goods and labor and time with the hope that the gods would make their lives better.

But you don't have to bow down before a statue in order to participate in perverse worship. Ecclesiastes reminds us that idol worship often takes a more subtle form. To the author of Ecclesiastes, the pursuit of money or power or any object of desire is the same as bowing before Baal.

Christians today face tremendous temptations to worship such idols of our heart. We go to church on Sundays, but during the sermon we think about how much better our life would be if we only had the money to buy our dream waterfront house or take that well-deserved island vacation. Even pastors may be tempted to worship at the altars of larger congregations, more tithing units, more honor and prestige.

And we, the authors, are no different than any other Christian. We too find our hearts wandering away from Jesus and toward other people or things that we delude ourselves into thinking can provide our lives with meaning and significance and success. Indeed, we have often kidded each other that this is our midlife-crisis book because midlife is a time to question what is truly important and Ecclesiastes speaks directly to these questions. But you don't have to be a midlifer to struggle with issues of meaning and purpose. No matter your age, we offer this book to you as an invitation to rediscover the abundant life that comes with putting Jesus in the center of life.

How can this happen? It starts with being brutally honest, admitting that much of our current activity involves "chasing the wind" or even after false gods and that it gets us nowhere. It starts with a deep dissatisfaction with the way things are and a hungry willingness to try something completely different.

Many voices in our day—through books, sermons, websites, media—are happy to tell us what to do. These voices, often solidly biblical, offer steps to guide us to a better world, an improved marriage, more obedient and culturally unaffected children and success in our work without losing our families. The trouble is, these steps often simply lay down a new set of expectations. Rather than merely feeling overwhelmed by the chaos, we also feel guilty for not managing it better. And we're still haunted by questions of purpose and meaning.

Ecclesiastes points to a different possibility—the possibility of real change. This comes when our hearts pursue a narrow way that at first seems more difficult than the problems we face. This new course of life sets the possibility for new decisions, new behavior and new meaning.

That possibility lies at the heart of this book, which follows the lives of eight fictional people as they confront their own questions of meaning and learn from their study of Ecclesiastes. The fiction chapters are intended to help you reflect on your life and the lives of your friends and family members. Interspersed with the fiction are sections that comment on the story and explore the major subthemes of Ecclesiastes. As in our earlier book *Intimate Allies*, Dan does the primary writing on the fiction chapters and Tremper does the primary writing for the nonfiction chapters.

At the end of each chapter, you will find a brief Bible study on Ecclesiastes as well as a series of questions for discussion and reflection. These materials can be fruitful for personal study, but we hope this book can also be a good resource for a small-group setting.

The book of Ecclesiastes is essentially a dialogue between two wise men—a skeptic and a person of faith. And for most of Ecclesiastes, the skeptic does the talking. He recounts his search for meaning in life. He explores the different idols he pursued to bring meaning to his life—control, relationships, work, pleasure, wisdom, spirituality, even life itself. His search ended in frustration, so he renounces all the effort he expended, warning his listeners that

- control will always slip out of our grasp.
- relationships will always disappoint.
- work will leave us frustrated.
- pleasure is always fleeting.
- wisdom is never an adequate guide.
- spirituality usually gives in to legalism.
- life ends in decay and death.

It's a disturbing message—and Ecclesiastes is not a book that most Christians enjoy reading. Yet it is the skeptic's bleak pronouncements that allow us to see through the fog of our hectic lives to the book's final conclusion: We find bold purpose when we submit to God's great desires for us.

Most of us at one time or another find ourselves tempted to move toward the worship of one of these seven idols, hoping to find joy, success and meaning. Ecclesiastes invites us to struggle against these futile temptations and move back toward God, the source of our hope. For if we allow ourselves to be disturbed and our idols challenged, we will find an essential and solid hope.

For in Ecclesiastes the skeptic's statements are not the answer. The ultimate answer lies in a paradox—that in losing our idols, we find not only meaning, but also God himself.

So as you read this book on busting the idols of the heart, rest assured. What may seem like a difficult premise—that we worship gods which are not God—can actually be a source of comfort. Our worship of other gods is not a new thought to Jesus. He is constantly being supplanted by his creation, yet he will be victorious in our hearts. He will win the supremacy he is owed. And he relentlessly undermines all that is not god to make room for the God who has redeemed our hearts.

1

CHASING AFTER POWER

"I Can Control My World"

✌

Noah pulled into the Brothers Consolidated staff parking lot to find his spot was taken. The interloper, a new kid who had recently joined the firm as a researcher, was just getting out of the car. Noah pulled up behind him and shouted, "When did you become a senior analyst?"

The kid jumped. "Hey, I'm sorry. Did I park in your space? I'll move. I'm really sorry."

"Consider it a gift today. Do it again, I'll have you towed—or give you an assignment that'll keep you here all night."

The kid kept on apologizing, but Noah had lost interest. He wanted to get his ducks in a row well in advance of today's meeting, where senior staff members were going to review their portfolios and reassess all their past decisions—including Pearson Furniture.

Pearson stock had recently dropped a few points on the NASDAQ and appeared to be sliding downward, but Noah believed the decline was just a minor blip in Pearson's progress. Pearson Furniture had recently lost a bid to place some of their products in a national chain of business stores—ostensibly because their line was not well developed and their offering incomplete. Noah believed Pearson's line was just ahead of its time—that the company was so good and so innovative it would soon dominate the business market.

Brothers Consolidated, of course, wanted the stock to fail so they could pick up *their options as it slid. Jonathan Satterwhite, Noah's chief rival, would argue with his usual suave confidence that his decision to select Pearson as a loser had been confirmed. But Satterwhite knew little about the personalities behind Pearson Furniture. He knew, as did everyone else in the business world, that the CEO, Scott Fitch, was an upstart, a jeans-wearing renegade. But Jonathan didn't understand Fitch's past, his personality or his passion.*

Noah did.

Noah had followed Fitch's life, studied his work, even talked with his senior staff. He had studied a tape of a talk Fitch gave his staff. The man had wept when he talked about a Pearson truck driver whose son had died of cancer. He'd expressed amazement at the man's heart to suffer for his son. Fitch was a hard-driving entrepreneur, but rather than talk to the staff about corporate policy or profits, he had shared what the truck driver taught him about life and then describing the kind of husband, father and friend he wanted to be—and what kind of company he wanted to build.

That speech haunted Noah. Not the tears, which he found maudlin, but the vision. The passion. Noah's instincts told him Fitch would use the rejection by the national chain to spur his troops on toward setting up a national business furniture wing under the Pearson name.

That stock was definitely going to rise. If Noah played his cards right, his stock in the company would rise as well.

Noah checked in with Janet, his assistant, then carried his binder and coffee cup into the sleek conference room. He took a seat next to Lee Reynolds, senior vice president of research and analysis for the Chicago office. Satterwhite, on the other side of the table, had already distributed copies of his report and opened his own leather binder, ready to begin his review. Noah skimmed the report quickly, then sat back, waiting for his moment.

Satterwhite launched into his usual smooth spiel. He quickly ran through the numbers and concluded crisply, "It's more than a good bet that Pearson will drop at least 20 percent over the next ten weeks. I think the market will be all over this in about a week, so we have only a brief window to take advantage."

Lee nodded, ready to move to another stock: "Any more discussion on Pearson?

It appears we have a winner here, and due to Jonathan's careful tracking, we may make this a great quarter."

Noah shifted in his chair, moving in for the kill. "Could I offer a minority view? I don't doubt Jonathan has done his homework, but let me ask him to give us his analysis of what Pearson Furniture has done with a few of its other setbacks."

Lee threw a concerned glance at Satterwhite, who shrugged. "Go ahead," the boss told Noah.

"Jonathan, are you aware of how Fitch handled the lawsuit that almost ruined his first start-up business? Or that he spent Christmas Day a few years ago loading trucks because they were behind on delivering their products after the storm tore through their distribution center?"

Satterwhite lifted his immaculately groomed eyebrows. "No, Noah, I'm not. I'm also not familiar with his psychological profile or his high school grades. But I do understand he is short and therefore may have a Napoleon complex."

The room roared with laughter. Round one to Satterwhite.

Noah smiled. He was not interested in winning this fight. He merely wanted to position himself as the lone dissenting voice. When the stock soared, he wanted to be remembered as the one who warned against betting the ranch on Pearson Furniture's decline—the who could have saved the firm a massive amount of money and avoided the wrath of countless investors.

Noah laughed. "I never thought to look at his high school grades, but I will. Until then, I do think that Fitch's track record in college ought to tell us something. He flunked out of three colleges and finally made it through after seven years. He then started four businesses that were eventually sold to his competitors because he beat the socks off each one of them in their key markets. The man is a wizard, and he thrives on adversity. I'm sure you're also aware there is no one better at pitching investment bankers. He has the uncanny ability to live with ambiguity until others bolt, then he calmly walks into the bank and takes the largest share of the prize. Let me play prophet. I think Fitch will . . ."

Noah laid out a scenario of what Pearson Furniture might do in the next six months. "If we want to make any profit," he concluded, "I think we should sell what we have now and then cover our losses by buying this stock to grow."

The room fell silent. Sweat gathered on Satterwhite's forehead, and he clenched his jaw. Lee gave him a somber look. "Respond."

Then Noah had the pleasure of watching his slick colleague scramble to defend his proposal. He managed to cover his lack of detailed analysis with a recitation of past successes, and the decision on Pearson eventually swung back to his side. That was fine with Noah. The doubt he'd wished to create sat squarely on the table, and no one would forget it.

On the way out, Noah walked by the kid who had taken his parking spot earlier in the morning. He grinned and complimented the kid's natty tie.

⅁

By the time Noah got home that night, he'd forgotten all about the Bible study. He hadn't even managed to read the first chapter of Ecclesiastes—and he hated to show up unprepared for anything. But he was stuck. He couldn't even trot out the "you can't believe the day I've had" excuse to keep from going; he had come home way too happy to pull off that one.

They ate a quick dinner at a restaurant near their house. All through the meal, Joan nattered on about Ecclesiastes. "I just don't understand why God allowed Solomon to do all the things that he did," she remarked as she forked up her salad. "I mean, how could he have had that many wives?"

Noah wondered the same thing, but for very different reasons. His mind flitted to the power of having a harem and picking a woman to be intimate with as casually as he would pick out a pair of shoes. He felt his breath quicken, but he knew better than to mention his thoughts to Joan. She would never understand.

After a quick supermarket stop, they found the apartment complex where Mark and Suzi lived, then meandered through the unfamiliar maze of driveways and parking lots before finally locating number 204 and snagging a parking space nearby. Suzi answered the door with her usual breathless giggle. "Hi, are you here for the Bible study? Of course you are." She accepted the proffered bottles of soda and motioned them into the brightly lit living room.

Noah blinked. The whole place was a riot of country kitsch—rag dolls, teddy bears, fake "antique" signs and plaques with cutesy sayings, scented candles with clashing aromas, and painted knickknacks on every conceivable surface. Noah did not know whether to laugh or smirk, so he concentrated on finding a corner where he could avoid having to converse.

Noah hated the first few minutes of small talk when walking into any gathering because he never knew who to be. If people saw him as the expert, he felt he had to be the Wise One and stayed aloof. Or if people saw him as a regular Joe, a nameless face in the crowd, then he endured the loneliness of insignificance and tried to ignore why he felt like a failure. In either case, he felt he could never win.

After far too long a time of forced conviviality, Jack convened the gathering. "Folks, why don't you grab your drinks, and let's get this ship out of the harbor." Jack began by introducing the new topic of the group's study. "As you know, we are launching into a new study tonight. I hope you will be as excited about studying Ecclesiastes as I have been in preparing for our time together."

Noah grimaced. Isn't it enough that I'm here? Now I'm supposed to be excited . . .

Jack continued, "With your permission, rather than go chapter by chapter through this great book, I thought we'd go theme by theme and see if we can zero in on the main points. I hope you all were able to read the book in preparation for tonight. What is the one word that kept sticking in your mind as you worked your way through it?"

Noah felt a tinge of guilt over being unprepared, followed by righteous indignation that such a demand had been put on a busy person like himself. He was relieved when Mimi Crawford broke the silence. "Meaninglessness," she said. "The book kept talking about life being meaningless."

Jack nodded. "Right, and didn't that strike you as strange? After all, as Christians, we know that God has given us abundant life now. But here is a wise man who seems completely depressed about the state of the world and his relationship with God. To be honest, I really didn't know how to take the book, so I started looking at some commentaries, and I read through the whole thing a couple of times. Fortunately, it's not too long."

Noah looked out the window at the passing traffic and glanced at his watch, calculating how long he would be forced to endure Jack's monologue before the group would be invited to pool their ignorance and give their opinions on the book. Jack kept talking.

"At first I was a little disappointed with the commentaries. They disagreed in their perspectives on the book, but they all pointed to the last few verses of the book—especially the last two verses—as providing the important teaching. Here, let me read those two verses to you, Ecclesiastes 12:13-14: 'Here now is my final conclusion: Fear God and obey his commands, for this is everyone's duty. God will judge us for everything we do, including every secret thing, whether good or bad.'

"Now, this seemed more biblical to me than 'everything is meaningless,' so I tried to understand the connection between the two. I went back to the commentaries and saw that the book really has two speakers. One is known as the Teacher; the other is known simply as the wise man. The wise man is the one who fears God and who concludes the book with a final perspective.

"If you look closely, you'll see that when the Teacher talks about life under the sun being meaningless—'under the sun' is his phrase to talk about life apart from God, life from the purely human perspective—he's speaking in the first person. You know, 'I saw this,' 'I did this.' But at the end of the book, the speaker is talking about the Teacher: 'The Teacher was like this,' 'the Teacher did this.' Those are some of the clues that two different voices speak in the book."

Noah glanced at his wife, who seemed enthralled. Noah wondered what would happen if he challenged Jack, but he couldn't remember enough about the book to offer another opinion.

Jack was studying his notes. "Now some people think the two voices are really the same person, and that was what I thought at first—that the Teacher was Solomon. I thought the book was written after he faced the foolishness of his youth, when he turned against God and started worshiping the gods of his foreign wives." He looked up. "I know this is a little tedious, but I think it is important."

Noah blushed and hoped Jack had not seen his yawn.

Jack pressed on, "I just have a little more. Some new commentaries, though, suggest that we are really dealing with two different speakers, neither of whom is

Solomon. The one in the main part of the book—the Teacher—is a jaundiced, skeptical old man who, on the basis of his observations of life, asks some very tough questions about relationship with God.

"The second is another wise man who wants his son, mentioned in the twelfth verse of chapter 12, to face the irregularities, apparent contradictions and unpredictability of life. The interesting thing is that the second wise man actually affirms many of the Teacher's observations. In fact, he does not reject any of the old skeptic's conclusions.

"This is a bit more radical than I prefer to admit. It seems like the last voice, the voice of the godly wise man, ought to contradict the Teacher's statements. But he never refutes the idea that life 'under the sun' is meaningless. He actually affirms those statements, using them to draw us to a brutally honest vision of life before turning to what is really important: fearing God.

"It's as if the second teacher is saying, 'Much of what you say is true. But you see only part of the picture. Your perspective is merely "under the sun." You need also to see what life looks like from "above the sun," from God's perspective.'"

Jack straightened up in his chair and looked more intently at everyone in the room. "I hope our reflections in this study will involve far more than mere commentary about what we think the book is teaching. I hope we can engage deep questions most of us would rather ignore. But I have to tell you—I feel a bit nervous about this book, more so than some of the other books we've studied. It makes me think in ways that seem out of step with my faith. I'd rather find answers rather than suffer the questions, which makes me . . ."

Noah wasn't listening. He was staring at Marcia's legs. She had shifted in her seat, and her tan, well-cut legs stretched out like an invitation to slip into a blue-green pool rather than sit in the hot sun of Jack's patter.

Marcia, Jack's wife, was neither young nor stunningly attractive, but her short, brown hair and her intense green eyes gave her a captivating, feline appearance. She was gentle and gracious, but Noah had noticed she held her own in discussions with quick wit and intensity.

Noah glanced over at Joan. Chin in hand, she listened raptly to Jack's spiel, though she probably had no idea what Jack was talking about. Noah let his eyes jump from one woman to the other, taking in the contrast. He loved Joan, but

Marcia—Marcia intrigued him. Though nearly ten years older than Joan and in many ways far less attractive, she exuded a kind of mystery that drew him to her. That and the legs—

"Is there anything on your mind, Noah? You seem particularly lost today in your own world."

Noah almost jumped at Jack's question but caught himself. "No, Jack. Sorry if I wasn't paying attention. I may have been wandering back to the slavish lusts of the day's business." The group laughed. Joan blushed. But Noah merely smiled and looked back at Marcia. For just an instant, she caught his gaze, then dropped her eyes and turned awkwardly toward Jack. It was the first time he had seen her lose composure.

Noah noticed a slight rise in Jack's chest, a tightening of his hands, a pinkish cast creeping across his left cheek. But Jack smiled. "Well, Noah, I suspect a whole lot more is going on in that sharp mind of yours than you are going to tell us." Noah looked at the Bible on his lap. He felt no pressure to respond to Jack's comment. He felt on top of things, in control. On the whole, it had been a good day, and he was eager for sleep. Sweet sleep.

Relieved when the Bible study was over, Noah walked to the parking lot slightly ahead of Joan. When he reached the space where he had parked the car, he found only a note held in place by a large stone.

The car was gone.

The note said: "Your car was parked in an unauthorized spot. It can be retrieved at the 285 Garage off Wadsworth and 285. Fee is $100—cash only."

𝕯

The Idol: "I Can Control My World"

We all tend to operate out of a faulty assumption that looks something like this: "If only I could control my world, life would be manageable and have meaning and purpose."

Related to that assumption is an equally faulty one: "I *ought* to be able to control my world."

Before you dismiss that last statement too readily, think about your life.

How much energy do you spend trying to manage your family life, your job, your life at church, your relationships? As you answer this question, you may come to realize you have sought the power to control your life with the passion of idol worship.

We all want control over the chaos of our lives. We don't like unwelcome surprises, and we plan and work hard to keep them at bay. We think ahead about the consequences of our actions, and we are not pleased when someone—a child, a friend, a stranger—disrupts whatever order we've established in our lives.

We often try to gain control through rules. Consider all the rules that govern our lives. We have our daily "to do" lists—laundry, food preparation, washing dishes, driving children to school, keeping our bodies in shape. At work, we have sales to make, forms to fill out, patients to see, classes to teach. We have rules of ethics, rules of behavior.

And there is nothing wrong with any of these rules—unless we let them rob our lives of passion. The rules can become demands that take away the depth, vitality and thrill of life. In pursuing the things we *ought* to do, we often lose track of what we *want* to do. The rules end up controlling us rather than helping us control our lives.

Our quest for control also tempts us to acquire power over others because we assume that power equals control. Power and control seem to be potential avenues of meaning in life; they give us joy and a feeling of significance. Experiencing the opposite, being pushed around by forces and people outside of ourselves, makes us feel our lives are ruled by chance and are therefore without meaning.

Noah is a good example of the way people attempt to control their worlds. Noah believes he is a Christian, but he really is a stock analyst; his job is his source of meaning. His passion is the hunt for information to make a deal that will not fail. He gives himself deeply to what provides him a sense of power and control over his life. He spends considerable time prowling the Internet and reading reports in his area of expertise. He loves the chase, loves winning over others.

Noah goes to a regular Bible study not because he wants to learn about the Bible, but because he wants to please his wife and do what's "right." He has taken on many of the values of religious people because it is easier to be on the side of the majority rather than to suffer the judgment of those with whom he might differ. And this arrangement seems to be working for Noah. He doesn't have to think in areas that trouble him. Instead, he is free to dabble in faith, know he has heaven ahead, and then focus his considerable talents on the real task: waging war at work.

Noah avoids what makes him feel uncomfortable. Like many men, Noah has found one area in which he excels, and he spends the vast majority of his waking thought and energy there. Consequently, he avoids his family and relationships in general. And when he is not at war in his work, he loves to sleep. In sleep nothing is required of him and life works, at least to a degree. Even Noah's sleeping is a way for him to control his world.

Is Control Bad?

It's not just Noah. Most of us live with the myth that we ought to be able to control our lives. So we work harder and plan more efficiently. Is that a bad thing?

No. Control is not necessarily a bad thing. Indeed, the Bible encourages us to exert control in several areas.

The book of Proverbs, for example, encourages us to plan for the future. Planning involves using our mental power in order to control what will happen to us. Planning is never precise and is always full of risks, according to Proverbs, but failing to plan is simply irresponsible: "Plans go wrong for lack of advice; many advisers bring success" (Proverbs 15:22). And when we submit those plans to the Lord, he will bless them: "Commit your actions to the LORD, and your plans will succeed" (Proverbs 16:3).

God wants us to plan. He wants us to think of the consequences of our actions. Generally speaking, no one can have a significant measure of success without foresight and the ability to affect the shape of the future.

The Bible tells us to discipline and control not only our own lives but also the lives of the people under our care. Proverbs reminds us, "Discipline your children, and they will give you peace of mind and will make your heart glad" (Proverbs 29:17).

Even more important, the Bible urges wisdom as a way to bring order out of chaos. We know from Genesis that as a result of the Fall, our world is wired for chaos. To bring an element of control to that chaos, we need wisdom. Helping us navigate through chaos is the whole purpose of the Old Testament wisdom literature.

Biblical wisdom is built on the premise that there is an underlying order to creation. God created the world; it is not the product of chance. Certain causes produce certain effects. If I go up to my wife and hug her, my actions will produce one desirable effect. Speaking harshly to her will produce a different and negative one. Different words and different actions will produce different effects.

To some extent, then, the Bible suggests, we can control how people respond to us. For example, when we encounter a fool, we need to know what kind of fool he is. Is he one who will act more foolishly if we take his arguments seriously and respond to his points? Or will he be one who thinks he is right if we do not answer him (Proverbs 26:4-5)? Once we determine these things, then we can give the most apt reply. "Timely advice is lovely, like golden apples in a silver basket" (Proverb 25:11).

The way of wisdom presented in the Bible, therefore, seems to support our desire for control. If that is the case, then the next logical step is to master wisdom, to learn the principles embedded in books like Proverbs, and then simply to apply them to the right situations. The book of Proverbs, after all, appears to be a list of insightful statements about how we ought to live life, a kind of divine self-help book that will take us through the turmoil of relationships and all the struggles of life. It offers a good, healthy kind of control.

The trouble is, not all our attempts to control our lives are healthy. And we can see that clearly in the Bible as well.

Abraham: Grasping for Control

In Genesis 12, God gave Abraham a series of promises that would shape his future (vv. 1-3). These promises include the fact that he would be the progenitor of a huge nation, a special people who would bless the whole world. For that promise to come true, however, Abraham needed a son. He and his wife, Sarah, were childless and growing old.

Abraham waited, but nothing happened. He began to doubt whether God would follow through with his promise. Abraham did not doubt God's existence, but he thought he needed to take steps to bring the promise to fulfillment. So Abraham took matters into his own hands. First he adopted Eliezer, his household servant, to be his heir (Genesis 15:2). Then later he took his wife's servant, Hagar, as a concubine and fathered a son with her.

All this was in keeping with the societal norms of the day. But God had specifically stated that he would provide the promised heir through Abraham's union with Sarah. When Abraham grew doubtful, he patiently repeated the promise.

But Abraham still didn't trust God. And the more he grasped for control, the more trouble he brought on himself. The family conflict that resulted from his efforts—especially Sarah's rivalry with Hagar—are well known. Indeed, once we take into consideration that Hagar's son, Ishmael, became the father of the Arab nations and Sarah's son, Isaac the father of the modern Jewish nation, we can see the level of chaos that resulted from Abraham's frenetic attempts at control.

Life Is Untamable

We are no different from Abraham. When we face a problem or an obstacle, we tend to take control and try to change it. But all too often, it seems, God has something different in mind.

Dan and I struggled with the area of control as we wrote this book. We spent a day in Denver to plot out our writing schedule—not only for the book at hand but for the next ten years.

As I left Dan's house to return to my home in Philadelphia, my sights were clear on what I had to do in order to accomplish the task of writing this book. Primed to get to work, I looked forward to the task with great excitement. I felt "empowered" and in control of my work and my life.

I got home from the airport, enjoyed a relaxing evening with my family, and headed to bed, anticipating the next day's work. At three o'clock the phone rang. It was my wife's stepmother. She sobbed, "Tremper, Bill just died!" It took a moment to register, but then I realized that my father-in-law had just passed away.

One phone call changed our lives for the next weeks. My writing schedule, my attempt at controlling my life, was seriously disrupted.

You have probably had similar experiences. Illness, financial upset, other people's decisions, and a host of other events can disrupt our well-laid plans. Such events remind us we can't really control our lives. But that doesn't keep us from exerting enormous energy to maintain the illusion of having life in order.

Think of Noah. He knows his business, and even though he doesn't win the skirmish at work, he believes he will win the war. He prepares and plots victory, and to a certain extent he is able to maintain control. But only to a certain extent—as the towing of his car reminds him.

While we can achieve a significant level of control, keeping all the plates spinning is no more possible than grasping the wind. That's one of the significant lessons of Ecclesiastes—that we must bow to the seasons of order and disorder God establishes in our lives.

The Teacher Questions God's Order

The book of Ecclesiastes contains a long speech by someone who simply calls himself the Teacher. He speaks in most of the book of Ecclesiastes (1:12—12:8). His words are framed by the words of another wise man, who assesses the Teacher's thought for his son—and for us, his readers (1:1-11 and 12:9-14). The Teacher sees life from a perspective that is "under the sun," that is, a solely human perspective (1:9, 14; 2:17; 5:18) as opposed to God's eternal, all-knowing perspective. And the general message of the Teacher's speech is that life is meaningless and our efforts at control are futile.

While the Teacher's comments about life will often shock and disturb us, if we are honest we will have to admit that his perspective often mirrors our own. Far too often we are frustrated with life because we are convinced that God is not in control and that he is leaving it all up to us.

The Teacher believed that God has created the opportune moment for everything. In one of the Bible's most moving passages about control and order (Ecclesiastes 3:1-8), the Teacher shares this perspective:

> For everything there is a season,
>   a time for every activity under heaven.
> A time to be born and a time to die.
>   A time to plant and a time to harvest.
> A time to kill and a time to heal.
>   A time to tear down and a time to build up.
> A time to cry and a time to laugh.
>   A time to grieve and a time to dance.
> A time to scatter stones and a time to gather stones.
>   A time to embrace and a time to turn away.
> A time to search and a time to quit searching.
>   A time to keep and a time to throw away.
> A time to tear and a time to mend.
>   A time to be quiet and a time to speak.
> A time to love and a time to hate.
>   A time for war and a time for peace.

We find comfort in those words, don't we? They remind us that everything has its proper place.

But here's the rub, according to the Teacher. Sure, God made the proper time for everything. He created everything for its proper place, and this is beautiful, but we can't know these times! We simply can never be certain that our words or our actions are right for the situation.

Immediately following the poem about time, the Teacher asks some unsettling questions:

What do people really get for all their hard work? I have seen the burden God has placed on us all. Yet God has made everything beautiful for its own time. He has planted eternity in the human heart, but even so, people cannot see the whole scope of God's work from beginning to end. (3:9-11)

God has created a world with order, and we yearn to experience that order. The Teacher tells us that this knowledge is beyond us all, and as a result we are frustrated to the core:

In my search for wisdom and in my observation of people's burdens here on earth, I discovered that there is ceaseless activity, day and night. I realized that no one can discover everything God is doing under the sun. Not even the wisest people discover everything, no matter what they claim. (8:16-17)

The Teacher touches the raw nerve of reality: The world is rigged for frustration. There is a right way to do things, but we will never know for sure what that is. There is a way to make life work, but we will never do it right. No matter how we try, we will never be in control of our world. It seems almost as if God asks our hungry souls what they want to eat, then prepares the food and places it behind an impenetrable glass wall.

Subjected to Frustration

In the New Testament the apostle Paul expresses the same truth: "For the creation was subjected to frustration, not by its own choice, but by the will of the one who subjected it, in hope that the creation itself will be liberated from its bondage to decay and brought into the glorious freedom of the children of God" (Romans 8:20-21 NIV).

The word Paul uses for *frustration* is the Greek word that is used in the Septuagint (the ancient Greek translation of the Old Testament) for the word *meaningless*, the word used most often in Ecclesiastes. In some English versions, this word is translated "vanity" or "futility." Paul's indirect allusion to

Ecclesiastes in the Romans 8 passage reflects his awareness that God deliberately imposes frustrations on us. He has made sure nothing in life will work in a way that allows humankind to think they are back home in Eden.

Noah experiences that reality. Though he basically feels that he rules his own life, he still has a few moments when he feels the sting of inner uncertainty. On the one hand, he hates to be the expert—that means accepting the pressure to perform flawlessly. On the other hand, he hates to be a mere mortal, a regular guy—that usually means living without praise or respect.

For the most part, Noah simply ignores an internal agitation that might signal a lack of control. When disruptions rise, he takes active steps to adjust to them and regain control. When traffic slows, he changes lanes. When the junior member of the firm takes his parking spot, he uses the situation to gain even greater control of the employee.

But even when we spend lots of energy wresting control from chaos, God will not let us achieve what would block us from himself. He actively orchestrates life so that we are continually presented with minor and major disruptions—and reminded that we are not in control. Noah experienced that too. The towing of his car reminds him that life is not tamable. God has rigged the world so that Noah's false sense of security will be exposed and his presumption of being able to control even the automotive aspect of his life will be upended.

Unfortunately, Christians often ignore God's disruptions, attributing them either to Satan's assault or just to the way life is. We too quickly mask our frustration, saying something like, "Well, I may not know what is going on, but at least God does!"

We assume God will take care of those who pursue him. We find ourselves attracted to sayings like "the LORD does not let the righteous go hungry" (Proverbs 10:3 NIV) rather than to sad—but accurate—observation like the Teacher's:

> The fastest runner doesn't always win the race, and the strongest warrior doesn't always win the battle. . . . People can never predict when

hard times might come. Like fish in a net or birds in a trap, people are caught by sudden tragedy. (Ecclesiastes 9:11-12)

The Teacher does not even find comfort in the idea of an afterlife where God puts everything right. As he looks into the future, he cries out:

This, too, I carefully explored: Even though the actions of godly and wise people are in God's hands, no one knows whether God will show them favor. The same destiny ultimately awaits everyone, whether righteous or wicked, good or bad, ceremonially clean or unclean, religious or irreligious. Good people receive the same treatment as sinners, and people who make promises to God are treated like people who don't. (9:1-2)

No wonder the Teacher concludes, again and again, that life is "like chasing the wind" (1:14 and many other verses). If we pay attention, we easily conclude the same. Even though we try hard, we can still feel we are groping in the darkness with no ultimate success.

People today spend a lot of physical, emotional and spiritual energy trying to control their schedules, jobs and relationships. We assume that the solution to our lack of control is to find new systems, new rules, new methods, new "laws" for doing things. We think that if only we have the right systems, we can control the chaos.

Our experience and the Teacher's observations deny this assumption. We need to turn from frenetically chasing control to something better. Under the sun, we chase control, but we discover it is as difficult to grasp as the wind. However, we can choose to move from an "under the sun" perspective to an "above the sun" one.

Let's take some time to explain this terminology, which will play such an important role in this book. We have already observed that the Teacher uses the phrase "under the sun" to describe life and perspective here on earth, apart from God. The Teacher himself never uses the opposite phrase. We are coining it to explain the opposite perspective. In other words, while the Teacher kept his search for meaning and truth utterly earthbound, we want to look at life from God's perspective as he reveals it to us in his Word.

How do we move from an "under the sun" perspective to an "above the sun" viewpoint? The answer, spoken by the second wise man to his son (and read out loud in Noah's Bible study), is simply this: "fear God and obey his commands" (12:13). Put God first in your life. If you want to find meaning and purpose in life, look at reality from God's perspective, not your own limited view.

Redemption Through Dependency

Our usual strategy for dealing with the mess of life is to seek control over it. We try to gain power in the world in order to have an effective platform to manage our existence.

Power makes us think of politicians and bankers, and most of us don't have that kind of clout. But power comes in gradations. We may experience the struggle for power in the family as we try to keep our kids in line or our parents from interfering. We may seek power in our community by doing volunteer work at the hospital or by running for a local office. We may seek power in our work by climbing up the corporate ladder, trying to become the boss so we can tell others what to do rather than have others tell us what to do.

Power—whether it is the power of status, abilities, career, position— ought to make us feel more in control. But we have seen that it doesn't. We can never tame life. As the Teacher woefully observes, "What is twisted cannot be straightened; what is lacking cannot be counted" (1:15 NIV).

The enigma is that it is God who has done the twisting and produced the lack: "Accept the way God does things, for who can straighten what he has made crooked? Enjoy prosperity while you can, but when hard times strike, realize that both come from God." (7:13-14).

So power does not bring control, and when we realize that, we are disappointed. We begin to feel that life has no meaning. We lose our vitality. The result is that we often give up any healthy attempts at control. We live half-hearted, passionless lives, letting events rule us, rather than the reverse.

Are these the only two options? Do we have to choose between a lifestyle of desperate grasping for control or a listless surrender to the mess?

Abraham: Receiving the Blessing

Let's return to Abraham for a moment. We have already seen him struggle with doubt in his relationship with God. We have seen him grasp at the promises that were at the center of his life and try inappropriately to take matters into his own hands.

But something happened to Abraham along the way, something that moved him from the struggle of earthly existence (under the sun) to a fear of God (above the sun). The change didn't happen overnight. Isaac's long-awaited birth was surely an influence, as was God's grace in overcoming many obstacles throughout Abraham's life. But by Genesis 22, which tells the story of the "sacrifice" of Isaac, the change in Abraham was clear.

After the promised heir was born, God asked Abraham to do the unthinkable, take this son and sacrifice him on Mount Moriah. We don't know what Abraham thought of these orders; he might have been angry, confused and afraid, but we do see his actions: obedience. He took Isaac to the mountain and surely would have followed through on God's instructions if God had not intervened and provided a substitute sacrifice.

Abraham had moved from an attitude of anxious chasing to one of divine dependence. He no longer tried to live life according to his own strength. Instead, recognizing his weakness, Abraham grew dependent on God. He found meaning and peace not by chasing after power, but by surrendering and trusting God.

Notice that the book of Ecclesiastes has the same message. The Teacher frets about the lack of control over his life. He cannot learn from the past; he does not know how to act in the present; he is frightfully ignorant of the future and paralyzed with fear.

The second unnamed wise man at the end, though, suggests the proper antidote. Don't fear your ignorance and lack of control, he tells his son; rather, "fear God." Submit your weakness and worries to the One who is truly in control, your heavenly Father.

Christ: Power Through Submission

We often lose sight of Christ's agony as he faced the cross. We often assume he faced his death with courage from the very start. But just before his arrest, he described the state of his soul as "crushed with grief to the point of death" (Matthew 26:38). The Gospel of Luke describes Christ's mental state as "in such agony of spirit that his sweat fell to the ground like great drops of blood" (Luke 22:44).

Christ asked fervently for the cup of suffering to be taken away from him. He really didn't want to go to the cross. But while Christ was tempted, he never rebelled against his Father's will. Rather, he submitted to him by saying, "If it is not possible for this cup to be taken away unless I drink it, may your will be done" (Matthew 26:42 NIV).

God's will took Jesus to the cross, a place of torture, shame and death. But it was the only way to the resurrection, an event of glory, victory and life.

Jesus is the One who shows us the paradoxical route to meaning in a chaotic and hostile world. It's the paradox of the gospel: Strength is found in weakness. Control is found in dependency. Power is found in surrender.

Noah fights hard to avoid this paradox. He believes, but he prefers a life that is not caught up in the struggles of Christ in the garden or Paul with his thorn in the flesh. And so do we. But God uses the frustrations of this life and the hurt of relationships to compel us to look beyond what we can control to the God who controls all things in order to woo us to himself. As we move from control to surrender, we move from chasing the wind under the sun to embracing God above it.

A Purposeful Life Above the Sun

From above the sun, we conclude that life under the sun was not intended to run smoothly. The road of life is bumpy and filled with obstacles—for everyone. This is the legacy of the Fall (Genesis 3). Life on earth is untamable. No human can control it.

And yet it is precisely in the untamable twists and turns that we actually meet God. We find ourselves compelled to surrender to his wisdom not when we feel strong and in control but when life careens off its expected course and we know we can't do anything about it. In these moments we are reminded that we have no control over our world. What we can control, however, is our willingness to seek God in the midst of seeming chaos.

When we are alert to God's working in our life, we can see how intrusions that overwhelm us, even those that are apparently evil, are his way of moving us toward something good. Surrender in this context is not an act of cowardice but an expectation that Romans 8:28 is true, that "God causes everything to work together for the good of those who love God and are called according to his purpose for them."

Once we adjust our eyes to see God in the midst of the apparent chaos, we can affirm that, although life is not tamable, it is purposeful—if we surrender to God's control and power. Surrendering doesn't mean that we spend less energy, but it does mean that we spend less nervous energy. We can live with a confidence that does not presume on our ability to rope life in but rather grounds itself in the strength and power of the One who made us.

Taking a Closer Look
Read Ecclesiastes 9:1-12.

1. Do you agree that sometimes chance trumps skill or ability?
2. Does life ever feel like a "net" to you (v. 12)?
3. What does this passage say about our ability to control life?
4. How does this passage effect your view of life when competence and skill seem to be bested by chance?

How Do We Chase After Power?

1. Over what parts of your life do you feel you have control? Where do you wish you had more?

2. What do you have to sacrifice to keep order in your life? Time? Relationships? Leisure?

3. What emotions do you experience when you feel that something is beyond your power?

4. Does the "power of God" have any practical value in your daily life? Describe where you see his power and how it affects your power.

5. How do you and your family plan your day, your month, your life?

6. What does it mean to you to surrender your life to God? What does that surrender mean for your planning?

7. Does the realization that life is ultimately untamable ever cause you to panic?

8. What verses from Scripture give you hope in the midst of panic or helplessness?

2

CHASING AFTER RELATIONSHIPS

"Relationships Bring Me Fulfillment"

Noah stared out the car window. The night lights twinkled and cast enough brightness to glimpse the kind expressions of Jack and Marcia in the front seat. Their easy patter made the ride that much more humiliating. Then Jack made the whole thing worse.

"While I have you captive in the car," he said, "let me ask what thinking you've done about Ecclesiastes."

The thinking he had done was less than zero, but Noah wasn't about to admit that. "Ah, well," he fumbled, "the book's point about futility feels fairly accurate. My day was going great, and then some idiot ruined it. So let me humble myself even more by saying I'm thirty bucks short of the fine to get my car back. Can we stop by an ATM or something?"

Jack smiled, "Don't have to. I'll spot you the cash. And relax. I can tell you don't ask for help too easily, but it's all right. We're glad to help."

Joan leaned forward. "You couldn't have said it better. Noah never asks for . . ." Her voice trailed away once she realized she had said more than Noah would appreciate.

But Noah wasn't even listening. He was looking at Marcia's eyes when she turned to talk—they sparkled even in the dark. Her voice suffused the car with a warm, calm reassurance. Noah sat back in his seat when he realized he was staring at her. Normally, he was a model of discretion—a conservative man, a paragon of moral values. But the contrast between Marcia and Joan made his chest tighten in frustration. He didn't want Joan to be lively and engaging; he liked her dull and predictable. But in Marcia's presence he felt drawn to a desire for passion that he usually allowed himself to feel only in his work. He would have to be careful.

"Hey, Noah, you seemed sort of preoccupied tonight. Care to talk about what you were thinking?" Jack was in that serious, caring group-leader mode again. Noah knew he couldn't evade the question with a witty evasion.

"I, uh, was lost in the day," Noah offered. "We had a huge meeting about a major stock offering, and I was pitted against most of the senior jocks. It was a fairly important Alamo for me if I am going to get the ear of the CEO. And I, uh, lost the battle, but I think if my instincts are accurate, I may have won the war."

Jack stopped at a traffic light and looked at Noah in the rearview mirror. "Noah, how long have I known you?" He gave his own answer: "About three years and two months if I recall accurately." Noah met the man's eyes in the mirror; he hated the way Jack was rarely wrong.

"So for over three years," Jack continued, "I have never once heard you talk like that about a business deal. You're usually a master of understatement; you minimize all your work activities. So I suspect all this talk about stocks means you're really thinking thoughts you'd prefer to keep to yourself."

Noah was glad the darkness concealed his flushed face. He felt exposed. For a brief, terrible moment, he even suspected he had been caught in his indiscreet thoughts about Marcia and his contempt toward Joan. But he quickly regained composure. "So now you're a shrink as well as a lawyer?"

Jack backed off. "What I'd really like to be when I grow up is a theologian. Then again, I like being able to fight over minutiae and actually make some money in the process as well."

Both men laughed, and the tension in the car relaxed as the play of shadow and light crossed their faces.

Jack started up the conversation again. "I know my mind is stuck on Ecclesiastes. But what amazes me about the book so far is how disruptive it is of every way we look at the world. I presume I know more than I know that I do, and I somehow think I can make my world work if I know more. Somehow those assumptions spill over into even my assumptions about all my relationships. For example, Noah, I presume I know you because we've been around each other for a few years, but it's just not true. I really don't know that much about you."

"I'm no mystery, Jack. But I guess I'm a lot more private than I realized. I guess, like most of us, I know myself the least. But I don't think I'm that difficult to know. Or maybe I am."

Noah yawned. He was anxious to end the evening and lose himself in sleep. But Joan seemed energized. She leaned forward and began to talk. "He does that to me a lot too. He doesn't really answer questions, at least not directly. And I end up making jokes, like you did, Jack. Or I just stare out the window and figure it's my fault for not being bright enough to ask the right questions."

The silence that followed hung heavy in the air. It seemed no one even wanted to breathe, let alone respond to Joan. The car jerked as Jack pressed on the gas in response to an impatient honk behind him. The light had turned green.

Noah turned to look at his wife, and his eyes flitted between a narrowing fury and a widening disbelief. He had never heard Joan so accurately describe his reluctance to talk about himself. Joan did not look at Noah. She kept her eyes forward, staring into the distance, again speaking to no one in particular. "I think Noah is happy to be alone. He likes being impenetrable."

If a person could fall off a car seat, Noah would have dropped to the floor. He had never heard his wife use a word like impenetrable. His heart began to beat fast; he feared that if he spoke he would reveal his panic. But if he did not break into Joan's monologue, she might say things that were best left to the pleasant vacuum he had thought made up his wife's inner world.

Noah jumped in before someone else could speak, "Whoa, folks. Before we get too psychological here, let's not forget we just got our car towed. So I'm in a bad mood and don't want to talk. It's no big deal."

"But it's true, Noah," Joan said quietly. "We've been married nineteen years, and I still don't know what you are thinking most of the time. I appreciate Jack asking, and I know you want the conversation to stop but I don't."

The car filled with a bright flash when it passed under the illuminated sign that announced their arrival at the towing service. In the brief exposure, all the faces in the car were taken back, except Joan's.

Jack drove through the entryway and into a parking place. Joan sat back, and a small smile crossed her face. Jack turned and said, "I know you're both tired, but thank you both for letting me ask a few questions. We like you both and would love to know you better."

Noah sat trapped in the back seat, unsure of how to answer Jack, furious at his wife but unable to let loose at her in that setting. He also felt oddly amazed at Joan's statements. He had no idea she felt left out.

"Well, Jack," he managed, "I guess we can say this has been a more true-to-life study than I thought it would be when we started the Bible study tonight. Thanks for the ride and for the extra funds. I'll get the money back to you the next time I see you."

Jack and Marcia opened their doors and moved the backs of their seats to let Noah and Joan climb out. Jack reached back and grabbed Noah's hand, drawing him out in a strong, swift move that made Noah feel like a child in his grasp. Jack smiled, and they shook hands. Marcia and Joan hugged.

The next few minutes were a blur as they paid a huge man with long, greasy hair and located their vehicle on a huge, shadowy lot. As they got into the Audi, Noah was already calculating how many minutes it would take to get home, check the phone machine, finish his e-mails, and then get to bed. But as soon as they were seated, Noah turned to Joan. "Cute. I did not appreciate your little pop-psychological analysis of me. I don't want that to occur ever again. Ever. Do you understand?"

Joan could not look at him. "I'm sorry, Noah," she said. "I got carried away. I guess I was thinking they were friends, and they were being so nice. And I was thinking during the study how often I just keep our lives under control by not rocking the boat or asking anything of you or anyone else. Anyway, it just kind of slipped out."

"Well, don't do it again," he snapped. "You know better than to carry on about our lives in front of anyone." He punched the radio on and started backing the car out of the slot.

⚥

Noah wouldn't talk to her.

He wouldn't look at her. He just stared straight ahead.

Joan leaned miserably against the door on her side as unwelcome memories washed over her. She was a nine-year-old girl standing at the car door, waiting for her furious father to finish fumbling with the keys to let her into the car after her second piano recital. And then, as memory skidded backward, she was walking up to the platform, heading for her turn on the piano bench.

She walked across the stage, took her place on the padded bench, and placed her hands on the keys. She paused an instant as she had been taught. Then she began to play. But after a few bars she realized the piece she was playing was not the piece she had learned. Other music kept sounding in the back of her mind, distracting her mind and her hands. Halfway through the piece the volume in her head increased drastically, and she fell silent, stunned by the vibrancy of the music in her head.

She stopped and stared at her hands. They would not play. Suddenly she was aware of the hall full of faces and the gasp that rose from the horrified audience.

She could not remember the rest of the piece. She took her hands off the keys and put them back into position. Concentrating hard, she began the piece again. But all she could hear in her mind this time was her father's furious voice.

His lungs were well developed after many years in the pulpit. Joan had listened to his scream countless times at the dinner table or in the car or before sending her off to bed. After awhile she had learned to detach herself from his anger. As his lips moved and his puffy face quivered in rage, she would allow herself to float into another world, where she heard only the smooth sounds of the classical music her mother listened to when her father wasn't home.

Joan liked the distant musical sphere. It was a safe space. No voices screamed. No one else could come in. She wanted to go there now, but all the sounds were confused now.

As Joan sat at the piano and listened to her father shout in her mind, her fingers played up to the bar at which she had stopped the first time. Then her hands stopped again. She couldn't remember a single note beyond that point.

This time when she stopped, she turned to the audience, gave a little smile, and shrugged. And an amazing thing happened. The audience—quiet, intense and straining for her victory—immediately relaxed and began to clap for her. The teacher bounded up the stairs and put the music in front of Joan. And that was all she needed. Barely looking at the sheets, she played a spirited ending to the piece. She even added a few concluding bars that were not part of the original piece.

She descended to the front row to sounds of applause and a sporting-event cheer from one older man in the audience. Part of her reveled in the acclamation, part of her dreaded leaving the stage. For she knew she would pay—for humiliating her father by making a mistake and also for garnering more applause than he had ever gained through his pulpit.

She found her parents in the crowd and then followed behind her father as they left. He moved briskly, barely speaking to some of the people who greeted him with a smile, a pat on the back, and some remarks about his daughter's sweetness.

Joan and her parents descended into the night. Her father's pace quickened. They walked in a straight line—her father, her mother and herself—all the way to their elderly Chevy.

After he found the right key and unlocked the car door, he yanked it open. He said nothing. He couldn't scream at her because some of the people in the parking lot were his parishioners, but she was sure he would hit her if he could. She peered beyond his furious face and listened hard for the distant music. Her heart moved toward it. Away from him—to a safe place.

The door shut, and she settled into the car. The radio came on, and Joan was shaken to realize she was not listening to her father's hymns. She was not in her father's car. She was in Noah's Audi, and Noah had just switched to a classic-rock station. The chugging guitars brought her back to the real world.

Joan looked over at Noah. He still stared straight ahead. She knew he would not yell at her or even ask a single question. He would stare out the window and count the minutes until he could be in bed.

She smiled to herself and thought about the recital piece she had not finished. She knew that piece—she could have played it backward if she wanted. She had just frozen because she couldn't decide to play it as written . . . because she heard something different. But was that so terrible?

In that moment something turned over in Joan's heart—a faint but distinct little click. The words she had read that day in Ecclesiastes seemed to echo with the music in her head.

Everything is meaningless . . . completely meaningless.

She had tried so often to be what Noah wanted her to be—and every time she'd failed. She had also failed to be what her father wanted her to be. She was the one the whole family treated like a slightly daffy child. But maybe, just maybe, she was a melodious child instead. A creative child who heard the music of other spheres, not the chords that most others heard.

Everything is meaningless . . . completely meaningless.

But what if meaning was just something you couldn't approach directly, as if life were a jigsaw puzzle that required mere perseverance? Maybe you needed something else—like sensitivity. Or imagination.

Joan's heart swelled with the hope that maybe life didn't have the meaning that Noah, her father, even Jack brought to it. The silly bantering of Noah and Jack, her father's puffy-faced rage, her mother's dutiful silence—maybe all that was what was meaningless. Maybe the audience's surprising applause, full of humanity in response to her sweet shrug, revealed a better hope than all the pious words and all the patronizing pats she had endured through her life.

Maybe. But in that lonely moment, the hope was more than she could bear.

The Idol: "Relationships Bring Me Fulfillment"

We often look to relationships to give our lives meaning. We yearn for closeness with friends, family members and people at our workplace or at school. We may think that if only we were married or if only we had a close friend, life would be so much better. Relationships are a hedge against loneliness, and some of us will do almost anything to gain friends and keep relationships harmonious. Our drive for relationship with other people can even become idolatrous, the most important thing in our lives.

And yet as much as we crave relationship, finding and maintaining good relationships can be as difficult as chasing the wind.

Consider Noah and Joan. Noah is an extraordinarily competent man in most areas, but in his intimate relationships he tends to fall short. He is involved with others when he needs to be, but the bridge to his heart is closed. He lives with a great hunger to succeed and an equally great commitment to make sure no one sees his inner world. So he spars with Jack. He is drawn to Marcia without really relating to her. He patronizes his wife. And he thinks it all works—until Joan breaks the silence with the truth.

Many relationships, even ones that have lasted for years, survive because the truth is left unspoken. To the degree that we live in silence with one another, we can feel the illusion of peace and even intimacy. Once we speak words that reveal disappointment, hurt or desire, then the tenor of the relationship changes. A new level of tension is introduced—and most people don't want that. They prefer conflict-free, undemanding relationships.

Noah is not terribly interested in the book of Ecclesiastes, except to make sure he is not exposed as a slacker or as biblically incompetent. He is not moved by the Bible study, though the inconvenience of having his car towed touches him deeply. His heart is moved not by his wife's loneliness, but by his own craving for peace, satisfaction and pleasure. His heart is far from considering truth in his marriage or the inner truth about himself.

Then Joan unwittingly opens up a hornet's nest. A meek and pleasant woman, she usually chooses not to engage in interactions that might cause conflict because she doesn't want to relive the sorrow, shame and anger of living with an emotionally abusive father. But on this particular evening, for some reason, she opens her mouth—and rocks their lives with her honesty.

It's the last thing Noah wants—but it may be the very thing he needs. For it is in relationship, especially our closest friendships and our marriages, that our lives will be most deeply disturbed . . . and drawn to the depths of truth about ourselves and God.

Can't Live Without Them

I recall taking our oldest son to college his first year at Clemson. I was overwhelmed with emotion as we hugged in his new dorm room before my wife and I left to return home. Alice and I were proud that our son had come to a point of independence, a point where he could leave home and begin to carve out a life of his own. Nonetheless, the sense of loss was almost overwhelming. We knew our lives would never be the same.

Relationships are crucial to navigating life successfully. Like all living creatures, human beings need water, food and shelter to survive. But we also need connections to other humans.

Think of the times when you have had a number of close friends and family members who have cared about you as you have cared about them. Then think of those dark times when you have found yourself without support, without someone who could share your heart. In the former times, life probably seemed vital, interesting, exciting, worth living. In the latter, life was probably dark, depressing, empty.

Because relationships are so important, the loss of a relationship represents a significant blow. In fact, the three most devastating events most of us in the Western world will ever undergo are a move, a divorce and the death of someone close. These are three quite different events, but the effect is the same. Relational separation is traumatic, whether it is an expected part of life, such as our son's moving to college, or an unexpected one, such as betrayal by a friend.

Relationships are obviously important to us, as vital as the air we breathe and the food we eat. Yet they can also be the source of our deepest questions and our darkest despair. If relationships are the route to meaning in life, they represent a difficult path.

The Gift of Relationship: Two Can Become One!

We yearn for relationship, the Bible tells us, because God made us that way. Our desire to know and be known intimately by another is not a perversion or sinful desire, but rather a God-given human trait.

According to Genesis 1 and 2, God originally created the first man, Adam, as a solitary being. He had an intimate relationship with his Maker, and he could relate to all the animals in the world that God had created. But God knew that this was not enough. Genesis records his divine acknowledgment and plan: "It is not good for the man to be alone. I will make a helper who is just right for him" (Genesis 2:18).

And he did! God created Eve, a being who could enter into an equal relationship with him. Who could labor with him to shape God's good creation into something even more beautiful. Who was like Adam but also different enough to draw forth mystery and a depth of intrigue that would require the two to spend eternity exploring the differences.

So we see that even before the Fall, the desire for an intimate relationship with another human being was a legitimate one, one that could not be satisfied even by an intimate connection with God. What an utterly remarkable, almost terrifying reality—that God made us to crave a relationship with someone else besides him. That's not the entire story, though—because God clearly intended that *both* people in a healthy close relationship would remain connected to him as well. This three-way relationship is at the core of our deepest psychological wiring: God, man and woman. When any link is missing, we experience a loss that has consequences for the soul.

The most dramatic relationship God gave his human creatures, according to Genesis 2, is the gift of marriage. This is the only human relationship that is exclusive. We can have many relatives, many friends, but only one spouse. And this is the only relationship that can take two separate people and merge them into one. Adam acknowledged this on the occasion of Eve's creation when he cried out: " 'At last! . . . This one is bone from my bone, and flesh from my flesh! She will be called 'woman,' because she was taken from "man."' This explains why a man leaves his father and mother and is joined to his wife, and the two are united into one. Now the man and his wife were both naked, but they felt no shame" (Genesis 2:23-25).

Further, the Scriptures are clear that this particular type of human relationship reflects in a special way our relationship with God (see especially Ephesians 5:21-33). Both marriage and the divine-human relationship are exclusive and totally vulnerable relationships to another person. Marriage mirrors our relationship with God as no other human relationship does.

But marriage is not the only human relationship the soul requires. The Bible also describes the deep need we have for other connections as well—kinship and friendship—to sustain us. Our hearts are wired for relationship; the chaos of life requires connectedness if we are going to survive, let alone thrive.

The very nature of being, in fact is wrapped up in the triple reality of *you, me, us.* I by myself am never enough. *You and me*—a pair—comes closer to what we were made to be, but a twosome without any other relationship or purpose eventually sours or loses its intimacy. The *us* is at least a third person and most likely a family, group or community.

But even these human relationships are not enough. We are still meant to relate all that exists on a horizontal, human plane to a vertical, supernatural realm.

God, after all, is the reason relationships are so important in the first place. Remember that God's very existence is essentially a relationship—Father, Son and Holy Spirit, bound together in deep love and unity for all eternity. And relationship is not only at the heart of God; it is the very foundation of the cosmos.

After all, God did not have to create the universe. And he certainly did not have to create other beings. But he did. He created celestial beings such as cherubim and seraphim. Most magnificently, he created beings made in his own image—he created humanity! And he did it all because he values relationships.

So again, the desire for relationship is not ugly. It is not a sign of weakness, but an important part of who God made us to be. In fact, fear or avoidance of relationship is an indication that something is wrong with us. All psychological pathology can be linked to the urge to flee or dominate relationships. And the person who is closed to relationships is equally closed to God.

The Triple-Braided Cord: The Solace of Friendship

Even the Teacher, who has little that's positive to say, recognizes the deep significance of relationships:

Two people are better off than one, for they can help each other succeed. If one person falls, the other can reach out and help. But someone who falls alone is in real trouble. Likewise, two people lying close
together can keep each other warm. But how can one be warm alone?
A person standing alone can be attacked and defeated, but two can
stand back-to-back and conquer. Three are even better, for a triple-
braided cord is not easily broken. (Ecclesiastes 4:9-12)

The verses immediately preceding this picture of the blessings of relationships show the pitiful nature of human existence by describing a person who
works hard to gain wealth but has no friends or relatives. To the Teacher, this
person is an example of the futile nature of life on the earth:

I observed yet another example of something meaninglessness under
the sun. This is the case of a man who is all alone, without a child or
a brother, yet who works hard to gain as much wealth as he can. But
then he asks himself, "Who am I working for? Why am I giving up so
much pleasure now?" It is all so meaningless and depressing. (Ecclesiastes 4:7-8)

It is in the light of this picture of the lonely miser that the Teacher turns
his attention to the benefits of companionship. What a blessing, in this hard
and hostile world, to have someone to share our struggles and problems.
And the concluding metaphor of the triple-braided cord suggests that two,
three or more companions provide even greater benefit.

Most interpreters of Ecclesiastes believe the Teacher is describing his own
struggles when he tells us about the lonely miser. That means his words
about the blessings of friendship are spoken with longing and desire. He
wishes he had such companionship in his life.

But we get the impression that even if the Teacher did have many friends,
he would still recognize their value was limited. As a matter of fact, when we
look closely at what the Teacher says, we see that his words are striking in
their lack of enthusiasm. According to the Teacher, though friends are a pos-

itive thing in this world, they certainly do not give life ultimate significance. Indeed, friendship, even when one can find it, often lets us down. It has a dark side.

The Dark Side of Relationship

The first few chapters of Genesis are foundational as we seek to understand our relationships. We have seen how Genesis 1 and 2 describe the creation of relationship and the joy and contentment that can be found in our marriages and friendships.

But if this is so, why are we so rarely content? Why are we lonely and frustrated in our relationships? If those first chapters of Genesis were the only Scripture we had, then it would not be true to the reality of our everyday life.

Theologians rightly call Genesis 3 the story of the Fall. It narrates humanity's fall from grace, from intimate relationship with God. Adam and Eve chose to rebel against God, kick against his authority and question his infinite wisdom. This immediately introduced a breach in their relationship with God.

But the Fall had a further result, one the biblical account emphasizes. It was only after they sinned that Adam and Eve felt shame, heartache and enmity with each other. Before the Fall, their union could be described as two people becoming one (Genesis 2:24). After the Fall, they looked at each other and headed for the hills. Their naked vulnerability became a source of fear and shame.

Physical and emotional nakedness is a wonderful thing. God created Eve so that Adam could look at her nude body and say, "Incredible! I desire to be intimate with her." The man's body was shaped in such a way as to exert a powerful attraction on the woman. To think that the naked human body is crude or to think that the desire to look at a naked body is perverse is essentially a criticism of God, the One who made us to please and desire one another in the context of relationship.

Remember, though, what happened after the Fall. Adam and Eve hid themselves from each other. Similarly, today, we withdraw emotionally. We cover up our inner feelings and resist truly knowing another person. In effect, we are still hiding "among the trees" (Genesis 3:8).

After the Fall, Adam and Eve were no longer intimate allies seeking to shape the Garden together. Instead, they became hostile rivals. We see this especially in the way they shifted blame to one another. Once God confronted them, Adam was quick to point the finger at Eve. "It was the woman you gave me who gave me the fruit, and I ate it" (Genesis 3:12).

Since then, no marriage or any other relationship has escaped the effects of the first humans' fall into sin. Though, as we will soon see, God gives hope for relationships, most intimate connections are marred by fights, abuse, neglect and loneliness. The two key issues that are played out in all relationships are *lust* and *violence*.

Normally, we think of lust as sexual—and it can be. But lust also involves a far bigger dynamic. It is essentially the compelling drive to get what we need and want by any means possible—to fill the emptiness of our souls through our own devices, without turning to God.

We all feel it—the painful void in the center of our lives. That inner ache is meant to drive us toward relationship with God. But too often we use it to justify rebellion. We turn away from God and look to fill our relational needs elsewhere. Lust is the dark intention to find an earthly lover—any person, object, or idea that will meet our needs, take away our pain and make us feel complete.

It doesn't work, of course. It cannot work. Obtaining the object of our lusts only leaves us more empty, more susceptible to shame . . . and prey to even hungrier desires. The very nature of lust is that it can never be satisfied.

The dilemma is that knowing God does not completely take away the emptiness, either. Turning to him can melt away much of our fear, loneliness and pain. But no relationship with God in this present world will ever be as rich, fulfilling or freeing as it will be in heaven. So we are left with a sense of incompleteness, what C. S. Lewis called our "inconsolable desire." Those who know God most deeply feel the inconsolable desire even more acutely.

This leaves us with a choice. We can point our inner emptiness toward

God, trusting him for our eventual fulfillment. Or we can make the decision to fend for ourselves, turning to false idols in our relationships, using or abusing others in the interest of getting what we think we need. Our lust, in other words, inevitably leads us toward violence in relationships.

Violence doesn't have to involve physical harm. It may emerge in words or body language, in our attempts to hurt or manipulate those who threaten us in some way. Treating another person with contempt is a violent act; it makes the other person feel small and worthless. The phrase "cutting a person down to size" gives an idea of the inherent violence in disdainful words and actions.

Lust and violence are closely connected. Lust describes our attitudes, our misdirected desires. Violence involves our actions, the things we do. We use violence to demand satisfaction from others and protect ourselves from perceived threats, to bind other people to us and blind them to what is true about us.

In this sense, Noah showed himself to be both a lustful and a violent man, though he didn't act out sexually and never raised a hand to the other people in his life. His greatest desire was to keep the upper hand, and he used whatever weapons he could muster—sarcasm, misdirection, outright anger—to thwart those who threatened him. His greatest satisfaction was showing up those who lacked the wisdom to see that their assessment of the Pearson stock was wrong. He hated their presumption and self-righteousness. But he was blind to the truth about his own harmful attitudes and actions—his hostility toward Jack, his fantasies about Marcia, his bad temper and condescension toward Joan.

Joan, on the other hand, lived her role of being a flighty, nonsubstantial person to convenient perfection. Her lust, or consuming desire, was for comfort and safety. Her passion was not to get something, which is how we often think of lust, but to escape any experience that triggered her painful past. She did not want to be yelled at or made to feel small by failing as she had done at the piano recital. And in her lust to avoid conflict and rejection, Joan too had acted violently, doing harm to her relationship and her own soul by withdrawing into her own little world. In pushing under her need for true intimacy, she diminished her relationships with others . . . until that night in the car, when her legitimate hunger for relationship finally broke through the lustful and violent reality of her life with Noah.

What Relationships Can't Do

Marriage is not the only relationship that has a dark side, of course. Other close relatives can be a source of pain. So can friends. Children learn this at a young age. On the playground they meet kids who play with them one day and turn on them another. They learn that friends can be cruel.

When we are honest, we realize that even our good relationships can't fulfill our needs for intimacy. Other people let us down. They use us, as the Teacher recognized in Ecclesiastes 5:11: "The more you have, the more people come to help you spend it." And we do the same thing to them. If we take a close look at ourselves, we realize we can't fulfill the needs of others. So our relationships become a prime breeding ground for anger and frustration, lust and violence and even idolatry.

I have a friend who constantly complains that her husband and children take her for granted. She does work hard to keep them happy, but her whole mental state depends on whether or not she gets the strokes she feels she deserves. If her husband and children don't affirm her in the right way, with the right gesture or the right word, she is devastated.

When we sinners come together in relationship, the problems intensify; they don't go away. We feel not only the frustration created by the inadequacy of another person but also the guilt of our failures as a spouse, a relative or a friend.

Perhaps no other area in our life raises more questions than our relationships. Perhaps no other area in our life causes more anger, jealousy, disappointment and stress than other people. The Teacher, though he had some positive things to say about relationships, recognized this frustration:

"This is my conclusion," says the Teacher. "I discovered this after looking at the matter from every possible angle. Though I have searched repeatedly, I have not found what I was looking for. Only one out of every thousand men is virtuous, but not one woman! But I did find this: God created people to be virtuous, but they have each turned to follow their own downward path." (Ecclesiastes 7:27-29)

Don't be distracted by the Teacher's attitude toward women here. His words are not meant to be a definite statement of what is right. They are being quoted by the second wise man, who uses them as an example to teach his son. Remember, too, that the Teacher reflects life under the sun and that he prizes men only a tad better than women. If the Teacher were a woman, she would probably say the same thing about men.

The main point is that relationships are unsatisfactory. And even when they are good, as the Teacher ruthlessly points out, they all end in death: "Whatever they did in their lifetime—loving, hating, envying—is all long gone. They no longer play a part in anything here on earth" (Ecclesiastes 9:6).

Our under-the-sun relationships can't supply us with ultimate meaning or purpose in life. Disappointments, rejections, betrayals, bereavements make this clear.

So what do we do? Should we adopt the devil-may-care attitude to which the Teacher resigns himself? "So go ahead. Eat your food with joy, and drink your wine with a happy heart, for God approves of this! Wear fine clothes, with a splash of cologne!" (Ecclesiastes 9:7). Or is there something more? Can we move from relational frustration under the sun to something better above the sun?

The answer is yes. But to understand how this works, we have to look beyond the Teacher's cynical proclamations or even the wise man's admonition to obey God's commands. We have to look to the gospel—and the amazing love of God himself.

Love of Self and Love of the Other

Why is it so hard to live in love and intimacy with God and others? The Bible's answer to that question is that deep down we love only ourselves. Love of self conflicts with loving another person. We want to be loved, but we find it hard to give love to another unless we get something in return. Indeed, we often give only as a way of filling our own needs. How often have we withdrawn from people to whom we have been close because we were getting nothing out of a relationship. How often have we wanted to be with another person because that person was making us feel good and was serving our own needs?

That kind of selfish love comes naturally to us. It's the ultimate source of the lust and violence that afflicts our relationships. But there's another way to live and to love, as the apostle Paul points out in the thirteenth chapter of 1 Corinthians. We often think of this chapter in the context of marriage, and indeed it is appropriately applied in that most intimate of human relationships. But Paul is really talking about attitudes and actions that should characterize all healthy loving relationships.

After asserting the importance of this alternative kind of love (1 Corinthians 12:31—13:3), Paul describes a heart that loves with passion and depth. First, the apostle tells us that love is patient and kind. It waits for the other, and it does so with concern, not irritability. It waits. It hopes. It loves beauty and justice and does not give in to the petty pleasure of seeing the one who hurt us stumble. Love is the Atlas of the soul; it keeps holding us up. It does not quit; it does not lose the memory of connection; it does not kill the dreams of reconciliation.

On the other hand, love wants nothing to do with jealousy or pride, which seek their own good at the expense of the other. Instead, love cares for the other, not for the self. Love does not keep accounts, weighing the advantages of a particular relationship. It is not based on what we can get out of a connection, but on what we can put into it. Instead it sacrifices safety ("I won't let myself be hurt again") and deals a death blow to self-righteousness ("After all I've done for them, I deserve better"). Love seeks the good of the other without denying the hunger of our heart or demanding that desire be satisfied.

It is this high call to other-centered love that strips us of any pretense that we love well. In light of the standard Paul describes, we fall woefully short. Yet, it is his vision of positive, unselfish love that allures our hearts to dream and fans our desire to grasp this kind of love. For it is in the midst of facing how little we love that we are drawn to the wonder of just how much we are loved by God . . . and the truth of how we can maintain the healthy, intimate relationships we desire so deeply.

Relationships Above the Sun

We desire intimate relationships. We want our marriages and family relationships and friendships to be vulnerable, supportive and warm, though they clearly don't always work that way. We know that part of the problem lies with us. At heart we are selfish people. The teaching of Paul leads us away from selfishness in our relationships and toward a love based on sacrifice, passionate regard and unselfish caring.

How can we manage such a love? Because of God's Spirit in us, we are drawn not only to Christ's example of sacrifice but also to imagine what love can mean in our lives. The Spirit warms our heart to love. He also deepens our awareness that our hearts ache for what only heaven can provide. In turn, the Spirit points our hungry hearts to the One who can both satisfy our hunger and empower us to live for love—Jesus Christ.

Jesus, through his amazing love for us, reestablished our relationship with God. He did it through the totally selfless act of dying on the cross. He gave his life for us so we can have an intimate relationship with God. He introduced us to his Father.

In the face of Christ we see the loving heart of the Father. He aches. He pursues. The Father relentlessly and with abandon seeks the lost even to the point of being willing to lose his Son to bring home his flock of straying, obstinate sons and daughters. It is through Christ we see the Father's desperate passion. It is God's warm heart that thaws my cold one and draws me to be willing to risk and sacrifice for love.

Christ's death not only creates a relationship with God, but also allows us to have meaningful relationships with other people. Just as the status of

Adam and Eve's relationship with God determined their relationship with others, so our relationship with Christ provides the foundation of our relationship with others.

The wild news of the gospel is that we can stop running after love because we have already been grasped by the Great Lover. We have been forgiven our sins, our consistent failures to love. We are free of all condemnation and have been invited to be to others what the Father has been for us all along: unnerving, persistent, passionate lovers.

The remarkable aspect of relationship is that the more aware we become of the inconceivable glory of being forgiven, the more we hunger to offer to others a taste of the same banquet. The more we see the pettiness and darkness of our hearts, the more aware we are of God's everlasting pursuit of our souls. It is then that we hear God's voice, which invites us never to forsake relationship, just as he has never forsaken us.

Putting God first in our lives helps us to see that we have only one certain relationship in which the other loves us unconditionally. Jesus Christ knows our ugly side, and he loves us anyway. Instead of recoiling from us, he moves more passionately into our lives. If we open our hearts to both his unfailing love and the certain failure of all other love, then we will no longer be surprised by betrayal, but will anticipate how it can deepen our love for Christ. And enjoying his love for us will always take us back into our struggle to love others, since he loves them as much as he loves us.

Our relationship with Christ is the footing that makes all other relationships not only possible, but even potentially rich. It even enables us to endure harmful relationships in which physical and mental abuse wreaks havoc in our lives.

After all, Christ loves us in spite of our rebellion against him. He has forgiven us, and that gives us the will to forgive others and move toward reconciliation. His love and forgiveness also gives us the freedom to recognize our own faults. What else could motivate us to do anything but look out for our own interests?

Looking at relationship from Christ's perspective (above the sun) gives us hope because we know that heaven will be a time of wonderful community, a time of perfect intimacy. The perfect relationships of Eden will be restored. It is from this eternal perspective that we are to endure all failures and betrayals. There will be a day of reconciliation for those whose lives are covered by the hope of the cross. Our deepest desire in relationship, intimate oneness, will be perfectly and gloriously fulfilled.

And even here under the sun, in our present relationships, all is not dark. We can't find our ultimate meaning here. But with Christ as our foundation, we can find some measure of fulfillment and support and even joy in marriage, friendships and other relationships.

The wonder is that the more these relationships grow, the more we come to understand what real love is really about. Only relationship with Christ can give us that above-the-sun possibility.

Taking a Closer Look

Read Ecclesiastes 4:9-12.

1. Look at the description of the value of the friend in this passage. Give examples of times when your friends have come through for you.

2. Have there been times in your life when you've been truly alone? How did you feel then?

3. Does this passage teach that friends are the most important thing in this world?

How Do We Chase After Relationships?

1. Think about the relationships you presently enjoy. Would you characterize them as healthy? Destructive? Nurturing? Abusive? Trusting? Suspicious? Supportive?

2. How important are your relationships to you? Do you consider yourself a social person? A loner? A family-oriented person?

3. Does God matter in your relationships? Which ones and how?

4. When a child grows up and leaves or a friend moves out of town or a

spouse goes on a short business trip, do you find yourself devastated? Why or why not?

5. Who do you usually put first in a relationship—yourself or the other person?

6. Would you consider yourself a jealous person or an indifferent person in relationships? If either one, why do you think that is the case?

7. What does it mean to have a relationship with Jesus? How does a strong relationship with him flavor your other relationships—marriage, friendship, children, business associates and so forth?

8. What Scripture passages help you anchor your relationship in Christ?

3

CHASING AFTER WORK AND MONEY

"Money Brings Me Freedom"

✍

The phone rang early and Joan turned over, only to find Noah's side of the bed empty. Normally, he would be just rising from bed and beginning his elaborate series of early morning rituals. But he was gone!

They had driven home the night before in silence. Joan had stared out the window, alternately waiting for the blast to come and sorely disappointed when Noah seemed oblivious to her presence. She hated his anger, but she hated being ignored even more.

The phone kept ringing. Joan stared at it, willing it to stop. But she reached over and silenced its irritating ring.

"Hello."

"Hi, Joan, this is Jessie. You know, from the Bible study?"

It took a long, uncomfortable minute for Joan to understand who was calling. She was still fogged with sleep and worried about why Noah had slipped away so early. She simply had no context for Jessie's voice.

"I'm—I'm so sorry, Jessie. Of course I know you. I should have been up earlier, but I just woke up. Sorry."

Jessie stammered as well. "Uh, no problem, Joan. I should have realized how early it is, but I'm off to work in a few minutes, and I just didn't think . . . It's just that Erin's sick—nothing serious, just a little fever, so she can't go to day care. And my backup sitter flaked out on me, so I either have to find someone to watch her, or stay home from work. And I wondered . . ."

Joan suddenly felt even more guilty. Not only had she not recognized the other woman's voice. She had also unknowingly rubbed Jessie's nose in the fact that she could sleep late, an option unavailable to a single mom. Jessie needed to keep her job at the Doggie Do Drop Inn.

Every time Joan thought of that name, she wanted to scream. Who in the world would be dumb enough to name a pet store the Doggie Do Drop Inn? Doggie Do. Oh, brother! But her irritation always moved to sadness when she thought of Jessie, who had told her story in bits and pieces at various Bible studies.

Jessie Drummond had been married for ten years to an alcoholic who sank deeper and deeper into his addiction over the years and become increasingly violent. Jim would get drunk a few times a month and go on a rampage at home. He rarely hit Jessie, but he did frequently break things Jessie valued. He would apologize profusely in the mornings if he actually remembered what he had done, but most of the time he acted as if nothing had occurred. And at church he always managed to keep up a good front as a deacon and leader in the men's ministry at their church. He was seen as a good man—warm, friendly, always helpful. Very few church members knew or wanted to know about his bouts with alcohol or his reign of terror at home.

Jessie had gone to the pastor and a few of the leading deacons to ask for help, but each time she had been told to trust God, remain submissive and encourage her husband to remain involved in ministry. "Sooner or later, Jessie," she was told, "God will get his heart. And it's best not to bring this up again because it will only tarnish Jim's reputation and cause more trouble for you in the long run."

When Jim finally left her for a woman he had met at a business meeting, Jessie had been relieved beyond words. She was finally free to live her life without the horror of wondering what would happen "next time." But a new sadness replaced her old fears. She had to leave her daughter at a day-care center. It broke Jessie's heart to see Erin cry as she left every morning. And the role of sole provider weighed heavy on her. Many mornings Jessie wondered if surviving Jim's rage and violence would be easier than working at a go-nowhere job.

Joan had picked up bits and pieces of Jessie's story over snacks on Bible study nights. *She felt terrible for her. So when Jessie asked hesitantly if she would watch Erin—"She won't be any trouble. You can just let her curl up in her sleeping bag and watch TV." Joan quickly agreed. At that point, she felt sufficiently guilty that she would have agreed to watch Erin even if she had had to postpone surgery or turn down an invitation to meet the queen.*

Twenty minutes later Jessie was at the door with Erin. The little girl stood there with her Big Bird sleeping bag draped over her shoulders while the two women chatted. Jessie seemed preoccupied and resolute. It was as if she had put on her work face and was preparing to walk into battle.

"I used to like pets," she said when Joan asked about her job. "Then again, I used to like people. But now I live for payday. That's why I have to be there today. If I don't show up, the boss will hold my check. He won't even put it in the mail, so I won't see it until next week." She sighed and tugged at a strand of hair that had escaped her ponytail. "Listen, I just can't tell you how grateful I—"

Joan cut her off. "Hey, I'm happy to do it. I just can't imagine all you go through in a day."

Jessie smiled. "It's worse. George, the boss is a letch—always hitting on the women in the store and giving us the eye. Once he dropped my check on the floor just so he could watch me bend over to pick it up." She made a face and stole a glance at her watch. "But enough of my soap-opera life. I've gotta run."

Joan and Erin waved as Jessie got into her brown, twelve-year-old Buick and drove off. Then Joan got the little girl nestled in her sleeping bag on the family-room floor and turned on the television. She still had a few minutes before the twins would be up, so she sat on the nearby couch and watched as a superhero flew in the air to rescue a woman who had just fallen out of a window. Does God do that—rescue people? *she wondered.* Or does he just watch little girls get sick and their mothers free-fall and then avert his eyes to avoid their sickening thud?'

She was shocked that such a strange thought had even occurred to her. But a lot of strange things seemed to be happening the past few days. For example, why hadn't Noah left a note or mentioned to her last night that he would be leaving early. Maybe he'd run away from home after the hassle with the car and the conversation with—

The phone rang again before Joan could finish the thought. It was Noah's assis-

tant, Janet. "Hi, Joan. Noah asked me to call you. He had an emergency at work. The report he made yesterday on Pearson Furniture caused quite a stir, and the brass have planned meeting in the New York office to go over his suggestions. Noah's on his way to the airport now, and he asked me to let you know. He'll be back late tonight."

Joan was stunned. She didn't know whether to be or grateful or upset that Noah had asked Janet to call. His assistant had never before relayed a personal message from Noah. Usually he just called on his cell.

"Thanks, Janet. I'll wait to hear the news." Joan went back to the couch and tucked her knees under her chin. Tears trickled down her cheeks. She didn't know exactly why. But ever since last night's Bible study and the conversation in the car, her life seemed to be sliding on black ice. She didn't get any traction, and there was nothing to be done. If she put on the brakes, she was sure she would spin more violently. So she just held on and waited to see what would happen next.

On the television the superhero was now wearing a suit and glasses. Somehow he looked much more like her vision of God: proper, well-groomed, distant.

She could not sit for long. She had to rouse Timmy and Ryan, get them fed and ready for the carpool, make a half-dozen phone calls, snag several service people, and run a truckload of errands. Well, the errands could wait. And she had planned to meet a friend for lunch, but she would cancel that in case Jessie didn't return soon enough to pick up Erin.

She picked up her dog-eared daily planner and looked over all the hours that were filled with mundane but necessary duties. Then she thought about Noah winging his way to an important meeting she knew nothing about. Why such a panic? Why such a quick demand to be in New York? He had to have known after he checked his e-mail last night. Why didn't he tell me?

Another tear escaped as she looked down at her scribbled list. So much to do— and yet none of it absolutely had to be done that day. No corporation would quake if her prognostications were right or wrong. If she chose to stay in bed, the twins would managed to fix their own cereal and drag their disheveled bodies to the corner to get a ride with Jimmy's mother. Even Erin would likely watch TV for hours and not need her to do a thing.

Joan was responsible for all the mundane matters that keep a home percolating along, but was her life crucial to anyone? If she just sat at the piano and did not finish the piece she was to play, what difference did it make?

Everything is meaningless . . .

The electricity in Timmy's room didn't work. She had to wait for the electrician, who had said he would come by sometime between one and four o'clock that afternoon. Her time was not that important; the electrician could have said that he would be there between Tuesday and Friday, and she would wait. It was her job. All the unpaid compensation—her room and board, the privilege of herding two rowdy but adorable little boys, the meaningful opportunity to sleep with a man who did not even bother to inform her he was going out of town—all that came with the one requirement: waiting.

Joan was a capital, first-class waiter. She waited on phones for credit-card personnel to clarify a charge no one in the house had made. She waited in line to pick up Noah's impeccably ironed, properly starched shirts.

The superhero made another bold leap into the air to save another damsel in distress. Why are so many women falling out of windows in New York? she wondered. Maybe they hate their jobs too and are either testing God or just giving someone else the chance to clean up the mess. At least the day wouldn't end in a fog of exhaustion and a sense of incompleteness that meant many of the penciled plans had to be carried over to the next day's endless trail of urgent but inconsequential tasks.

Joan rarely allowed herself to think about her life. She found it too disturbing. She had learned through her father and the daily drudgery of life that it is better to focus on the task at hand, not meaning, not desire, and certainly not her pain.

She looked at Erin, tucked away in the yellow sleeping bag, sucking her thumb, her brown ponytail tied back with a fuzzy green band, lost in the televised flurry of danger and rescue, good and evil.

The two of us are just alike, *thought Joan.* I'm just as wrapped up in my little world as Erin is in her cartoons . . . and mine makes about as much sense.

𝕯

He'd done it again—and once again, she'd had to take it.

Jessie's face flamed as she reached for the phone to tell Joan that her manager had pressured her into working late . . . again. He stood behind the counter with a barely concealed smirk as she struggled to hear over the furious barking from the grooming "salon."

The Doggie Do Drop Inn—or the Doggie Do, as the employees called it—offered a combination of grooming services, pet supplies and upscale boarding kennels. In other words, it was a strange combination of a Southern beauty parlor, retail store and animal jail, all with clever names and higher-than-average prices. And Jessie Drummond was like all employees who there—ashamed of the name, worried about job security, and perpetually irritated by the mind games George Banta played with all the employees, especially the young or unmarried women.

George was clever enough never to cross the line of propriety in public and provoke a charge of sexual harassment, but he pushed the limit with his double entendres and leering once-overs. Jessie had grown accustomed to being used by her husband on command and under conditions that made George look like a choirboy. But listening to George's "compliments" about her hair and the neckline of her dresses felt like walking with a stone in her shoe. It was possible to continue, but at the same time the distraction and numbing pain made the journey almost unendurable.

Jessie had thought about slapping him, reporting him or quitting. But each time she reached that point, she would picture Erin and know she was stuck. She knew she would not be able to find a better-paying job without a college degree or at least some technical training. So she always resolved to be smarter, quicker. She wouldn't be caught alone with George the next time. She wouldn't let him take advantage of her.

But then it would happen again. Because she needed the job, her boss had power over her, and he knew it.

Why did she have to work and be humiliated when all she wanted was to provide for her child? All she wanted was to be treated with respect, and all she got was mindless work and demeaning sexual innuendo. She didn't know if it was because she was a divorced woman . . . or merely a woman.

All she knew was there were no safe places.

🖎

At three o'clock Jessie called Joan to report apologetically that she had to work overtime in the warehouse. Her voice, which sounded frantic, could barely be heard over the sound of barking, and Joan thought she heard someone laughing in the background. She assured Jessie everything would be just fine.

Jessie responded, "Yes, Joan. Someday it will. Thank you."

Jessie's voice made Joan want to cry, but she held back her tears. "Take your time. Erin and I will be here when you get done at work."

Joan had spent the day watching Erin watch television. She could not even recall if she had made lunches for her boys. Somehow they had gotten off to school. All the phone calls, errands and other to-do-list demands had been lost in the meaninglessness of the day. She liked the little girl's company, enjoyed hearing her laugh. At one point she even considered crawling into the Big Bird sleeping bag beside her but decided that would be an unlikely fit.

When the phone rang again, Joan jumped off the couch to get it. All day long she had expected Noah to call. She caught her breath and tried to slow down to sound as normal as her racing heart would allow. "Hello."

"Hi, Joan. This is Jack."

"Jack, I . . . I was not expecting you."

"No problem. But you sound a little breathless. Am I calling at a bad moment?"

Joan hesitated, unsure of what to say. Then she blurted out. "It's just that . . . Jack. I haven't heard from Noah all day, and he left this morning so early I didn't get a chance talk with him. I'm afraid. I'm afraid about—"

"Last night," Jack spoke with quiet intensity.

"Yes."

Jack must have leaned back in his desk chair because Joan could hear the squeak and groan of the swivel. His voice was reassuring. "Joan, I'm not surprised, but obviously I'm disappointed. I had prayed Noah wouldn't turn on you. I may have been out of line in asking those—"

"Oh, no," she answered quickly. "I'm really glad we had the discussion, though I really don't know what to do about his not calling me. He actually had his assis-

tant call to let me know he was flying to New York. I didn't have any idea where he was."

Jack exhaled, "I'm going to call Noah this week and see if we can have lunch or something before the next Bible study. Marcia and I wanted you to know we'll be praying for you both."

Joan didn't know what to say. She looked down at the multicolored pad of paper next to the phone. It was blotched with tears, and she hadn't even known she was crying. Somehow she managed to thank Jack and hang up without bursting into sobs.

Joan walked back to the couch and saw Erin had fallen asleep. She looked at the TV, hoping against hope that the caped crusader was still rescuing women falling out of windows. She so wanted to see him rescue someone.

The Idol: "Money Brings Me Freedom"

Our advertising-heavy culture screams at us in countless ways that if only we have enough money, life will be meaningful. We look to money to bring us security, freedom, pleasure and power. As a result money easily becomes an idol we worship in the hopes of getting our needs met and our desires fulfilled.

Most people spend nearly half their waking life commuting to and from work or actually on the job. As e-mail, faxes, beepers and cell phones proliferate, our work week seems to expand. With such demands on our time, our work can easily come to command our whole attention. But work means different things to different people.

Noah loves the challenge of his work, the thrill of the hunt and the satisfaction of the kill. He is good at what he does, driven to succeed and well paid for his efforts. His job is also a significant source of meaning and power for him.

Jessie's life, on the other hand, reveals the dark side of work. She earns just enough to survive, and she feels stuck and victimized in her job. She is untrained and ill equipped to meet the challenges of the twenty-first century.

She knows she can be easily replaced. Consequently, she feels compelled to endure the abusive conditions of her job—a boring routine, meaningless interactions and demeaning intrusions that make her life miserable. For Jessie, work is a labor of survival . . . and of love. She endures daily degradation for the sake of her daughter. But she derives little satisfaction from the work she does.

Joan's work situation is somewhere between the other two. Her work as a stay-at-home mom is unpaid, most often unappreciated, usually noticed only if it's not done . . . and her feelings about it are ambivalent. She loves her kids and likes the freedom of not having to go out to work every day. But the routine and isolation of her situation sometimes overwhelm her; she feels lost in mundane, routine tasks. The sense of emptiness is complicated by the fact that her husband loves his work more than he loves her. She envies Noah's freedom, his sense of power. Yet when she looks at Jessie's life, she thanks God she does not live that kind of a trapped existence.

Why We Work

Most people fit somewhere between Noah and Jessie. We may live for work, feel ambivalent about our situation, or hate our jobs and work solely to survive. And let's be honest—money is a concern for all of us. After all, we need money in order to eat, to put clothes on our back and a roof over our heads.

The trouble, whether we earn minimum wage or pull in a six-figure salary, is that we always feel just a little more would be enough. But when that little more comes, it seems to run through our hands so quickly we feel we are trying to grab the wind.

And many of us yearn for our work to provide more than money. We also crave challenge, enjoyment, a sense of purpose. And because we invest a lot of our lives in what we do for a living, we naturally hope to find meaning and purpose through it. We want our work to *mean* something.

As a professor at a seminary, I have met many devoted men and women who have left lucrative careers because they are not happy with their work in spite of the high pay. They desire more than money; they want to make a difference in the world. Some of these people, as devoted as they are, go into the ministry and are surprised to find that their work life is still filled with frustration. The sense of fulfillment they expected to find in the ministry seems to be as elusive as wealth itself.

Work, money, wealth. They are important to us and take up large chunks of our time and energy. It's not surprising that the Bible and, in particular, the books of Proverbs and Ecclesiastes, have much to say about these topics.

The Value of Money and Work

Most people think the Bible frowns on wealth. They commonly quote the saying, "Money is the root of all evil," forgetting the verse actually says, "The *love* of money is the root of all kinds of evil" (1 Timothy 6:10, italics added).

Nowhere does the Bible say that the rich are heading toward perdition simply by virtue of their wealth. Indeed, many Bible "heroes" were fabulously rich people—for example, Abraham, Jacob, Joseph, David, Solomon and Joseph of Arimathea. Job was an exceedingly wealthy man for his day. And though God took away his wealth in order to test him, he also provided him with even greater wealth afterward.

The Bible condemns wrong attitudes about money, in other words, but it never says that wealth is bad and poverty is inherently good. The book of Proverbs, in fact, actually affirms the opposite:

The wealth of the rich is their fortress;
    the poverty of the poor is their destruction.
The earnings of the godly enhance their lives,
    but evil people squander their money on sin. (Proverbs 10:15-16)

Wealth makes many "friends";
    poverty drives them all away. (Proverbs 19:4)

The wise have wealth and luxury,
    but fools spend whatever they get. (Proverbs 21:20)

The Teacher of Ecclesiastes also acknowledged that wealth gives people authentic enjoyment and is something to be desired. In Ecclesiastes 7:11-12, he talks about how wisdom is superior to money, but he does so in a way that, far from denigrating money, recognizes its value:

Wisdom is even better when you have money.
> Both are a benefit as you go through life.
Wisdom and money can get you almost anything,
> but only wisdom can save your life.

And then hear what he says in Ecclesiastes 10:19:

A party gives laughter,
> wine gives happiness,
> and money gives everything!

There have been periods in church history—especially during early and medieval times—when money, like sex, was considered to be inherently evil. Those who followed God were supposed to be both poor and chaste, and the monastic life was considered the ideal of great spirituality. Remnants of these ideas continue down to the present day—but they are not really biblical. They reflect Greek philosophy, which separated the body and the spirit.

According to the Bible, however money is not evil. It is a necessity and a blessing from God—and working hard to make a living is a virtue. Indeed, the Bible's harshest warnings are directed toward the lazy. Paul tells Christians to "Stay away from all believers who live idle lives and don't follow the tradition [of work] they received from us" (2 Thessalonians 3:6).

Work was originally a gift from God, an important part of the world he created for Adam and Eve before the Fall. Genesis 2:15 states this clearly: "The LORD God placed the man in the Garden of Eden to tend and watch over it." Work was a God-given responsibility that human beings were to enjoy and from which they were to derive satisfaction.

The picture of work that we get from Genesis 1 and 2 is an extremely positive one. Adam and Eve labor together to develop what God has created.

They have orders to "govern" the earth, to "reign over the fish in the sea, the birds in the sky, and all the animals that scurry along the ground" (Genesis 1:28). It is their job to "tend and watch over" the beautiful home that God has given them (Genesis 2:15). And they do it together, in harmony with each other and with God.

Indeed, in their work, Adam and Eve were reflections of their Creator. The Bible opens with a magnificent portrait of God the Worker. Through his Word, he brought the cosmos into existence and put both time and care into shaping it into a thing of great beauty. God intends our labor to involve the same energy and creativity he exhibited when he created the cosmos. He intended it to be beautiful and fulfilling, not a source of boredom or humiliation, frustration or failure.

Why then is our experience of work sometimes so difficult, its results so often unsatisfying?

The Futility of Work

I write these words as someone who passionately enjoys his work as a teacher and a writer. I often can allow work to consume more of my heart and soul than it deserves. Indeed, I find it hard to contemplate anyone's relishing work as much as I do. However, even those of us who like our work must honestly acknowledge its frustrations.

Just yesterday I got a small reminder of the pain of labor. I was writing this section about the irritations and setbacks of work when my computer screen went blank. I had been working on my laptop computer out on my porch, using battery power. I knew that I might run out of power, but my computer automatically saves the file before it switches off. Under normal circumstances, though, it gives me a message that the file was saved. This time no message appeared, and I was left staring at an ominously empty screen.

Holding my breath, I quickly got the adapter cord and plugged it in. I turned the computer on and was greeted by a harsh grinding noise and blackness. My heart sank.

Hours later, after the battery was completely recharged, the screen flickered on. But when I searched for my file, I discovered that my morning's work had vanished into cyberspace.

Disappointment changed to anger. I had wasted a whole morning of valuable time! But then I remembered the topic of my writing. What else should I expect? Work, far from always being a source of joy and fulfillment, can be fraught with obstacles and frustrations. And the book of Ecclesiastes acknowledges this, articulating and explaining the feelings we have on a daily basis. The Teacher did not anticipate computers or the computer demons that can snag a day's labor. But he did understand that all our work can quickly turn to dust and our efforts can be impeded by a world that doesn't easily respond to our touch.

The Teacher also recognizes that much of our working effort is driven by envy, the lust to have what others possess. "Most people are motivated to success because they envy their neighbors" (Ecclesiastes 4:4). This is a staggering truth. We see a coworker or a boss getting more money, more perks than we get, and we set out in hot pursuit to gain the same advantages. The kind of envy that the Teacher describes here is extremely destructive since it encourages people to get what they want at the expense of others.

In addition, the Teacher notes that those who have the right motives don't always win. "I have observed something else under the sun. . . . The wise sometimes go hungry, and the skillful are not necessarily wealthy. And those who are educated don't always lead successful lives. It is all decided by chance, by being in the right place at the right time" (Ecclesiastes 9:11).

This observation about life in general has obvious implications for our work. No matter how gifted, prepared and honorable we are in carrying out our labor, we have absolutely no assurance that our work is going to be rewarded, financially or in any other way. Life is often run by what appears to be brute luck. One person stumbles onto good fortune; another works a lifetime and doesn't seem to get a break.

We want to scream, "That's unfair!" or "It can't be true!" But we can see it in our own workplaces. Lazy, unworthy, or unprincipled people often prosper, while those struggling to serve God and help others often suffer. No wonder we envy those who succeed.

The Teacher does not say that the violent *always* prosper or that the godly are *always* held back. He would admit that it is possible to be righteous and to do well, though he would probably suggest that it is rarely the case.

But even occasional prosperity would not make the old cynic happy or relieve his anxiety. He wants us to know that the frustration of work can go even deeper than failure, that success itself can be unfulfilling.

> So I came to hate life because everything done here under the sun is so troubling. Everything is meaningless—like chasing the wind. I came to hate all my hard work here on earth, for I must leave to others everything I have earned. And who can tell whether my successors will be wise or foolish? Yet they will control everything I have gained by my skill and hard work under the sun. How meaningless! So I gave up in despair, questioning the value of all my hard work in this world. Some people work wisely with knowledge and skill, then must leave the fruit of their efforts to someone who hasn't worked for it. This, too, is meaningless, a great tragedy. So what do people get in this life for all their hard work and anxiety? Their days of labor are filled with pain and grief; even at night their minds cannot rest. It is all meaningless. (Ecclesiastes 2:17-23)

The Teacher presses the point further than we are likely to do in our daily lives, but he is certainly right. Even if we work hard and with integrity, we will one day die, and there's always the possibility that our heirs will waste or squander what we leave behind. So any kind of success in this world carries a measure of frustration with it.

The Power of Money

One of the chief motivations for going through the agony of work is the need to get money. Meeting our essential needs does not require a great deal of money. But even when we have enough food to sustain our bodies and adequate shelter to protect ourselves from the elements, we usually want more.

Why? Because money provides protection and empowerment. It provides us with the means to fend off assaults and helps us control our lives—up to a point.

Just this week, my father had major heart surgery. But he almost didn't get to the doctor on time. The cardiologist he was supposed to see never returned his phone calls to schedule a catheterization. Finally, my mother asked another cardiologist, a friend, to intervene. When my father finally went in for the appointment, the cardiologist determined that he needed to have surgery within the next few hours! The unreturned phone calls almost killed my dad.

The whole situation made us all think. What would have happened if my parents had not had a friend with connections and health insurance to pay the bills? What about poor people who have neither?

The truth is, money directly influences the way people treat us. Jessie lives out this reality on a daily basis. She feels powerless because she cannot afford to report her lecherous boss. She might lose her job. And even if she eventually gained legal redress, she would not be able to survive financially in the meantime.

Jessie is not alone. The majority of humanity live daily with the bitter reality that the lack of money increases our chances of being ignored or exploited. The reverse is also true: money also makes it more likely that we will be well treated. My wife has noticed, for example, that department store clerks treat her better when she is wearing an expensive outfit than they do when she is wearing jeans.

This kind of financial discrimination happens even among Christians—as the New Testament writer James pointed out. He noticed that believers were more welcoming and supportive of well-to-do visitors than they were of those who came from the lower strata of society. He rightly reprimanded the church for this unfair treatment (James 2:1-13).

James reminds us of our natural, though sinful, human tendencies. We may envy or resent people who have more than we do. But consciously or unconsciously, we also admire them. People are attracted to the rich. They want to be around those who have money. Thus, one reason we desire money is that we want people to pay attention to us and give us the best treatment. Money helps make that possible.

The Futility of Money

Money is a powerful thing—an avenue for distributing blessing and curses. No wonder we want more of it. A number of motivations drive us: fear, anger, the desire for independence, the need to control others. And that is why, in the final analysis, we feel that we can never get enough money. Because while wealth is a blessing and reward, it simply cannot provide everything that we expect of it. Wealth can never fully protect us, provide us with love, or negate the effects of the Fall.

The Teacher speaks frankly about this when he laments:

> Those who love money will never have enough. How meaningless to think that wealth brings true happiness! The more you have, the more people come to help you spend it. So what good is wealth—except perhaps to watch it slip through your fingers! People who work hard sleep well, whether they eat little or much. But the rich seldom get a good night's sleep.
>
> There is another serious problem I have seen under the sun. Hoarding riches harms the saver. Money is put into risky investments that turn sour, and everything is lost. In the end, there is nothing left to pass on to one's children. We all come to the end of our lives as naked and empty-handed as on the day we were born. We can't take our riches with us. . . . People leave this world no better off than when they came. All their hard work is for nothing—like working for the wind. (Ecclesiastes 5:10-17)

In these verses, the Teacher specifies a few reasons why money never satisfies, no matter how much we have, and why we're always craving more. For one thing, people latch on to rich people and take advantage of them.

Those who have money must be hypervigilant against those who might target them for their money.

A close friend of mine lives in a wealthy part of town and has found that service people often raise their prices when they see the size of her house. She ends up having to pay more for the same quality and quantity of work that other people get. It's hard for the middle class and the poor to feel sorry for the rich, but this does illustrate the Teacher's point that increased income results in increased expenses.

The Teacher knows well that hard-earned money can also quickly evaporate. In a single day, for instance, a dramatic stock-market shift (or a fire, hurricane, or death) can bring huge losses. If anything, the Teacher reasons, money brings worry, not security. The working poor sleep well; the rich toss and turn, wondering about their fortunes.

Though money is necessary and powerful, it can never brings ultimate satisfaction. It can prove to be a false ally and can bring disappointment, even despair. Thinking otherwise can lead to great pain and even tragedy—especially when we let it become an idol. As the apostle Paul points out, "some people, craving money, have wandered from the true faith and pierced themselves with many sorrows" (1 Timothy 6:10).

Restoring Work Through God's Glory

There seems to be no direct correlation between money and fulfillment. I saw this recently on a ministry trip to Mexico. Most people outside of Mexico know the Acapulco of glittering beaches, sunny skies and luxurious hotels. But over the mountains that conveniently shield the rich is the real Acapulco, with around one million people living in poverty. During the trip I found sad, lonely people in the rich hotels and confident, happy people living in shacks. I also saw the opposite. That trip made it clear to me that money isn't what determines a person's love or hate of life.

We have to look at work and money not only in the light of our creation, but also through the prism of the Fall. After all, Adam and Eve's sin had serious and explicit repercussions for our work life and our enjoyment of

God's good creation. We see this specifically in the words that God speaks to
Adam after his sin of rebellion:

> Since you listened to your wife and ate from the tree
> > whose fruit I commanded you not to eat,
> the ground is cursed because of you.
> > All your life you will struggle to scratch a living from it.
> It will grow thorns and thistles for you,
> > though you will eat of its grains.
> By the sweat of your brow
> > you will have food to eat
> until you return to the ground
> > from which you were made.
> For you were made from dust,
> > and to dust you will return. (Genesis 3:17-19)

These indeed are harsh words, but they ring true to experience. We know
the sweat and difficulty of working to eke out an existence, the labor that it
takes to enjoy creation, the ultimate sense of futility. God warned the first
human couple that if they sinned, they would die (Genesis 2:17). He gave
them (and us) life, and he is perfectly just in taking it away as well.

In all of this, God is not cruel, but just and abundantly gracious. Indeed,
because of our sin, death became a reality—but not immediate death.
Though life and labor remain difficult, they also included many elements of
beauty and satisfaction.

But that is not the end of God's grace. For after the Fall, God did something totally unexpected. Almost before the Garden gate had slammed shut
on fallen humanity, dooming us to painful and futile labor, God embarked
on an audacious plan to remedy the situation. At great sacrifice to himself,
he provided a way out of the mess.

As the Old Testament unfolds, this plan of redemption takes on clearer
and clearer shape. Isaiah speaks of this redemption as something that costs
us nothing!

For this is what the LORD says:
> "When I sold you into exile,
> I received no payment.
> Now I can redeem you
> without having to pay for you." (Isaiah 52:3).

And in Isaiah 55:1-2, the appeal goes out:

> Is anyone thirsty?
> Come and drink—
> even if you have no money!
> Come, take your choice of wine or milk—
> it's all free!
> Why spend your money on food that does not give you strength?
> Why pay for food that does you no good?
> Listen to me, and you will eat what is good.
> You will enjoy the finest food.

The message here is that we don't have to work to earn a place in God's heart; we don't have to pay money for his love. And that message came to its greatest fruition, of course, in the coming of Jesus. The riches Christ gave up for us far surpass the riches of money or material things. And the riches he provides for us provide the true wealth we need for above-the-sun living.

The Bottom Line

Work is important in this world. Money is important. But the bottom line is that as long as we strive to find our satisfaction and purpose in work or money, we are doomed to a life of meaningless futility. We are built for Eden, after all. Billions and billions of dollars cannot be enough for those of us who have been ejected from God's Paradise. We can never be happy with anything short of restoration to the Garden, and only Jesus can provide that.

Our work in a fallen world will always frustrate us if we make it an idol. Whenever we depend on money and work to shield ourselves from cruelty, sorrow, loneliness and need, we will run up against the futility of labor under the sun.

But is this the final word? Of course not. God has a good purpose for our struggles with work and money. But first he wants us to face our illusion that we can find any level of real happiness in what we do or how much we earn.

The message is the same through failure or success: no "it" is enough. Work is an "it." Money is an "it." Both involve objects and the process of acquiring objects. But acquiring things is a slippery slope. The more you get, the more you want. The more you want, the more dissatisfied you feel when you can't get it.

Money and work expose the depths of our depravity. Like relationships, work and money satisfy us initially but then leave us disillusioned, hungry for what no person or object can give us. That's why Jesus taught, "Don't be so concerned about perishable things like food. Spend your energy seeking the eternal life that the Son of Man can give you. For God the Father has given me the seal of his approval" (John 6:27).

Among the fascinating people that my wife, Alice, and I met in Acapulco were Willie and Bruni Bezemer. Willie works at the luxurious Princess Hotel as the head pastry cook, a prestigious job. While Willie was giving us a tour of the hotel and showing us many of his wonderful edible creations, he told us the story of his life.

For many years, Willie poured himself into his profession, working hard to achieve his international reputation. Though his wife was a Christian, he was more interested in cultivating his jet-set lifestyle. When he heard that the fabulously wealthy Howard Hughes was taking up residence in the top two floors of the hotel, Willie thought he had reached the crown of his career. He would create the most fabulous baked goods for the wealthiest man in the world.

When Hughes arrived at the hotel, he ordered a cinnamon bun. Willie did the work himself, using the best ingredients and giving the order his best attention. He sent up the pastry with great expectation, only to have it returned with the message that it was inadequate. Willie sent another, but again Hughes rejected the creation. After Hughes sent back Willie's third attempt at creating the perfect cinnamon bun, Hughes sent his private jet to his previous place of residence to retrieve an example of the type of cinnamon bun he wanted. When Hughes' servant brought Willie the bun, he couldn't believe his eyes. It was a piece of junk, the type of bun that anyone could pick up at a grocery store.

This experience brought Willie's world crashing around him. His life, which was wrapped up in his work, had no meaning. His years of dedication to his craft seemed to have no purpose.

But God had a purpose beyond anything Willie could imagine. Willie's crisis opened his eyes to Christ's love, which he saw displayed in his wife's love for him and for other people. After a time of questioning and exploration, Willie found his satisfaction in Christ. After that happened, he once again found joy in his work.

Purposeful and Redemptive Work

Once we begin to grapple with our illusions about work and money, you see, we can pursue our daily labor in a way that leads to personal change and perhaps a measure of satisfaction. God's intention in work is to draw forth our sense of godlikeness in the joy of creating, making and shaping.

In a fallen world, this joy is never complete. We always bump up against futility. But even futility is not the end of the story. Futility can serve the positive function of keeping us from making our work and money into idols. Our sense of futility also draws our hearts to the basis of true riches—Jesus Christ—and to the greatest work of all time—his labor of dying to pay our penalty of sin and rebellion.

This attitude can lead to an anticipation that asks, What is God going to do today in my work? How will he unnerve me, expose me, allure me, use me, bless me through my labor? We may always be ambivalent about our work—hating it and loving it—but at least it will arouse us to look to the heavens to ask the question: God, what are you doing in my life?

After all, we now know that our work is not the most important thing in

the world. If we falter in our work, we are not complete failures. God loves
us whether we are poor, middle class, or rich.

This does not mean it is wrong to work hard for a good salary. But at the
same time, we are to strive for contentment with what we have. We may pursue a better job or a raise, but if we don't get it, we should never become
angry or bitter. In the words of the Teacher,

> Enjoy prosperity while you can,
>> but when hard times strike, realize that both come from God.
>> Remember that nothing is certain in this life. (Ecclesiastes 7:14)

More important, our love of God and gratitude for what he has done
should drive us to concerns that transcend our needs and even the needs of
those nearest us. One of the surest signs of the heart's redemption is the desire to bless others with the fruit of our labors.

Why Are You Working?

Our ultimate goal, after all, is not to become financially independent or to
be the richest person in our community. Our goal is to hear these words
from our God: "Well done! . . . You are a good servant" (Luke 19:17).

One of the most basic decisions about work is this: Do I work for *this*
world, or do I work for the world to come? As the Scripture has made clear,
there is nothing wrong with being rich, wanting more money or working
diligently with a thoughtful plan. The question is simple: Will I work for
myself or for God?

We are not to work for power, protection, or the pleasures of this earth;
we are to work for the words "Well done!" Desire for our Father's blessing is
to be the sweet, alluring energy behind all our labor.

Even the middle ground of saying, "Well, I'm working for my kids' education" or "I'm working for our retirement so we are not a burden to the
kids" or "I'm working for a small piece of the pie and a few earthly pleasures"
can easily become a smoke screen to avoid the more basic issue of whether
we are working for ourselves or for God.

One way to determine for whom you work is to ask yourself this question: Do I pray, plan and perspire in my work to make more money so I can give more away? As you see needs in your community, do you ache to earn more to help a poor child enjoy a week in the country and purchase a computer to join the world of knowledge and competency? Are you driven to earn more so that you can help a needy neighbor?

Don't misunderstand us here. It is not wrong to dream about getting yourself a new fly-fishing rod, a new car, or a new piece of furniture. None of these objects is inherently wrong; each can be used redemptively for God's purposes. But work and wealth have one true, eternal purpose: to invite others to know God.

One man I know threw a staggeringly lavish Christmas party in order to attract his extremely well-to-do neighbors, business associates and friends to join him in celebration. He also invited a few people from different countries, races and socioeconomic settings to talk about their Christmas experiences. The wealthy guests were enchanted by the cultural diversity represented. What they weren't prepared for was having the African American pastor talk about the poverty, heartache and confusion of having to grow up with a white Santa who didn't deliver presents to his home.

When white guilt in the room was at its apex, the pastor shared that Christmas is not about Santa but about Jesus, who is neither black nor white, who was a helpless Jewish baby born to a poor family in a setting of squalor, with no future but to flee from the hatred of the ruling class. The pastor passionately described that Jesus' goal was to die for all of us who are humble enough to cry out like the rich tax collector: Help me.

My friend gives his hard-earned money to bless the poor and the rich, the hungry and the well fed. And that should be our purpose too. Money provides a way to give blessing and eventually to gain the one blessing our souls are most craving to hear: "Welcome home, my son, my daughter. Well done."

Work and Money Above the Sun

In life under the sun, we never have enough. But this is the way life is supposed to be. If we were satisfied, we would not long for something better, something that can be satisfied only in heaven, that is, above the sun.

Once we have adopted this above-the-sun perspective, our work and money fall into proper perspective. We will no longer hate our work, even though it frustrates us, because work is not where we find our ultimate meaning. And we will not work for our boss, our company, or even for ourselves, but ultimately for the glory of God. This is as true for those in sales as for those in the ministry; it is as true for the homemaker as for the missionary. All work has eternal significance.

Work also provides the venue for us to reflect our Creator. We are created in God's image, meaning that we have creative impulses that can be applied to our work as gardeners, janitors, parents, counselors, politicians, ministers, students, accountants, pilots and pet-store workers.

Money above the sun becomes a tool not for filling the void—it can't, since we were made for Eden—but for enjoying God's creation and extending his kingdom. And since money doesn't purchase what is really important, we can hold it more lightly, with far less worry and anxiety.

This brings us back once again to Ecclesiastes' command to "fear God and obey his commands." Our fear of God informs us of what is really important. As long as God is the most important thing in our lives, money and work take a proper subordinate significance to us, engendering a contentment with what we have and a generosity toward others

Our vocational and financial realities will inevitably involve frustration, sacrifice and loss, but the Bible teaches us that even small sacrifices today have eternal ramifications. We have left the riches of Eden and have been cast out into the wasteland. But we look forward to the restoration of Eden and, indeed, to a place that will make the Garden look bare (Revelation 21—22).

Taking a Closer Look

Read Ecclesiastes 2:17-23.

1. The passage describes how hard work leading to monetary success can

be frustrating. What kind of satisfaction can money lead to?

2. Can you think of real-life examples of wealthy people who have died sad or angry?

Read Ecclesiastes 5:10-17.

The passage describes how money can lead to frustration. We can all agree that money is necessary to live in the world and that we must work for it. Is it possible to recognize that reality and still find contentment? How?

How Do We Chase After Money?

1. Take a moment to assess your money situation. Would you consider yourself rich? Poor? Getting by? Are you content with your present financial situation, or do you find it an occasion for anxiety or even panic?

2. Are you hopeful about the future in terms of your financial security, or are you depressed? Why?

3. Take a moment and assess your work situation, whether that work is outside the home or in it. Are you content with your work? Do you enjoy it or hate it? Why or why not?

4. Would you consider yourself a workaholic? How would your spouse or close friends characterize you?

5. Is your chief motivation in your work to earn money to survive? To thrive? To gain prestige in the eyes of others? To help others?

6. In what ways do you relate Christ to your financial and work situation? In what ways do you tend to keep your finances and work separate from your spiritual life?

7. How can finding your ultimate meaning in Christ help you have a more balanced perspective about money and work?

8. What Scripture passages can help you maintain that balance?

4

CHASING AFTER PLEASURE
"Pleasure Will Satisfy Me"

The next two weeks melted into a routine of early-morning departures. Even Noah's nighttime routines were disrupted. Many mornings he never bothered to let Joan know whether he was going to be late, and many nights he simply went to bed without even reading his usual few pages of a financial quarterly.

And day after day, he spoke only if Joan or one of his sons asked him a question. She blamed herself for Noah's silence or anger—she didn't know which it was. She just knew that one unplanned, inadvertent conversation in a car seemed to have changed her life.

One morning Noah had made a remark that hinted his job might be on the line. Joan knew better than to ask for details. She found herself checking job offerings online in case the unthinkable happened. But she was more frightened at Noah's silence than at the prospect of having to go back to work.

One morning when Joan walked into the closet, she noticed that Noah's travel bag, his best suits, and several of his most expensive starched shirts were gone. She immediately looked to see if he had packed his shaving kit. It was gone as well. Her heart sank. Her mind began to race. Was he leaving her? She could not even conceive of Noah having an affair, but she couldn't think of another explanation.

It was the longest morning of her life.

Just before lunch, Joan called Noah's office and was put on hold. She waited, her hand quivering. Several times she almost hung up. Finally, a familiar voice came on the line. "Good morning, Brothers Consolidated. This is Noah Adamson's office. How may I help you?"

"Ah . . . hi, Janet. This is Joan Adamson. Is Noah available?"

A long pause was followed by a hesitant response: "Joan, I'm sorry. Noah is in New York. He left on the six o'clock flight to La Guardia. He will be in meetings all day. Do you want me to have him call you? He should be calling in for his messages sometime this afternoon."

Joan's pulse beat loudly in her ears. She heard the question, but she could not speak. She could not ask Janet to remind Noah he had a wife.

"Yes, please have him call," she finally managed, and hung up before his assistant could reply. If he were in meetings, he probably wouldn't answer his cell phone, and he would more likely get the message from Janet than if she left a message on his phone.

The day swung between the mundane errands that for brief periods enabled her to forget Noah and the dark moments when Joan's imagination got the best of her. Just before dinner Noah finally called.

"Hey, babe. Noah." In nearly nineteen years of marriage, Noah had never used any endearments, let alone called her babe. Not that babe was endearing, but it was a huge stretch beyond his normal, clipped greetings.

"Hey," he continued, "I'm real sorry I didn't—hold on, Gary, I'll be with you in a minute—I didn't let you know what was happening. But I was too tired to tell you about this trip last night when I found out I had to be in New York. Anyway, the meeting is going to stretch on through tomorrow. I had a flight home, but it isn't going to work. So—hey, Gary, hang on; don't leave me here. I don't know where we're eating. Sorry, Joan, but we're heading out now to eat and drink away the day. Don't worry. They're drinking; I'm their designated taxi hailer. The meeting is still a tossup. I'll either be the goat or the hero. At the moment, I have sprung horns, and if I keep talking and making the big boys wait, I'll have a full-fledged tail. I'll call you when I can. Bye, hon."

Joan put the phone into its cradle. Hon. He had never called her that, either. Was he drunk?

Or was he talking for someone else's benefit?

❧

Noah's head felt light. He knew the conversation with Joan was bizarre and unlike him. He had postured to hide the tension between them from his compatriots. He hung up the phone and turned to look at the three men in nearly identical gray suits. They were differentiated by their ties. Their tan faces marked them as successful and sophisticated players in the game of life. They stole occasional glances at Noah; they were either anxious or furtively hiding their patronizing pity. He could not read them. If he could interpret their fleeting looks, then perhaps he could determine whether he was going to have a job tomorrow or be out on the street.

The meeting had basically involved six hours of territorial marking. The eight big dogs in the room, including the two men who owned Brothers Consolidated, had spent the first few hours analyzing Noah's report on the Pearson Furniture deal. Figures glided around the room like streaking pigeons, only to land a few feet further away from their original pecking point. Then another flurry of financial spreadsheets would be scattered by one of the big boys.

Noah knew he was the interloper—the Chicago hotshot analyst who had stirred up trouble. His analysis of the Pearson stock had involved a level of psychological profiling that had never been utilized at the Brothers and it had caused a stir with the Andrajian brothers.

The firm had been established by the brothers, two Armenians who had come to the United States soon after their parents had been killed in one of the least-known and least-cared-about holocausts. Money for them was not a matter of wealth or privilege, but a bulwark against future holocausts. They were notoriously cautious about innovations. And no one in the meeting wanted to risk his privilege by challenging a system that had been established by the brothers and had worked for twenty years to produce one of the strongest, most successful stock firms in the country.

Noah had known he was taking a huge risk when he proposed getting rid of the Pearson stock. But he had not understood the extent of the peril or the weight of the cultural stream into which he had chosen to throw his small, flat-backed stone. After six hours, he still could not tell whether the stone had skipped effortlessly to land on the other side of the stream or had sunk at the first touch of the water.

What he did know was that he could not decline to go out to eat and get a few drinks with his three compatriots. After a day of posturing and plotting, he was absolutely required to go out to the watering holes of the city to do the same. At least he would be able to take his coat off.

He wanted desperately to go back to his room at the Four Seasons and crawl into the womb of his bed. Instead, he would follow the flow of money and conversation to learn how to proceed during tomorrow's jousting for place and power.

He wondered what Stephen and Sam Andrajian would do this evening. He could never understand why they insisted that their employees stay in one of the most expensive hotels in New York City while they stayed in the same small room at the Algonquin, a writer's hotel full of history, dark corners and the ghosts of Hemingway and Virginia Woolf.

"C'mon, Noah, it's time to go float your boat. We're going to let you decompress after that marathon," said James McKenna, the head analyst over the entire Andrajian empire. "Well, ol' boy, you were fairly subdued after your initial report. What were you doing? Watching us flap about to make sure you were there at the end like a vulture to pick up the pieces? You certainly were a man of few words after you dropped the bomb. But we'll see tomorrow where the buck stops." James laughed with a hearty but ominously textured roar.

The evening was spent over a multicourse meal at Il Mulino, the best Italian restaurant in the city. Five waiters hovered over the delivery of hors d'oeuvres, fresh olives, breads of Olympian glory and salads that would make even the sophisticated Epicureans swoon. The wine steward had been told to provide for them with little regard to the cost. The first wine cleansed the palate. Their second wine announced the arrival of a decadent repast that could neither be finished nor allowed to be scraped into the holding bin for uneaten food. The whole meal was exquisite torture, a culinary seduction that could not be resisted even if one were tied to the mast as the sirens began to serve pasta.

By the time the main course arrived, Noah had forgotten about the day. He had forgotten about Joan, the awful phone call. He had even forgotten about the day ahead. Pleasure had erased his past; it had expunged his future. For the first time in a week, he felt free and happy. Noah nipped at his fourth glass of wine. He was not unfamiliar with imbibing, but tonight he consumed far more than normal.

The intense interactions of the last few weeks, from his initial Pearson presentation and Joan's disruptive conversation in the car with Jack and Marcia to the flurry of meetings and trips, faded slowly—as did Noah's focus. He looked at his watch and noticed that he had to stare with intensity to distinguish the small and large hands on his watch.

The evening passed with convivial jocularity and a fair amount of boasting about people, places and privileges. Noah was quiet, but he laughed more than he had in a long time. These men were larger sharks in the dark eddies of work, but out on the town they were expert conversationalists and fascinating storytellers. For Noah, the mealtime passed like a few hours in a hammock.

The group finished their meal, and after tipping everyone from the waiters to the chef to the maitre d', they walked two blocks east to the Blue Note, a popular jazz spot. The streets were ablaze with the cacophonous harmonies of the Village. Noah walked behind the other men and stared at girls whose body parts were pierced with stones that glittered in the night air like constellations. The fragrance of the cool breeze, the sensuous bodies and the alcohol-induced euphoria led Noah to a joy that he seldom encountered other than in sleep.

The remainder of the evening was a blur of the music, drinks and conversation. Noah did not even remember when he got back to his room or how he undressed or if he called the operator for a wake-up call. Pleasure had endowed him with an Elysian holiday, and he lingered there as long as he could—until the inevitable morning light awakened him to inescapable reality.

⚅

Joan looked at her two boys stretched out on the carpet, heads on the crunched-up sofa pillows she had told them a thousand times not to use, staring blankly at seventies reruns she has asked them not to watch. Today, she didn't care. She had dinner to prepare, and her day of mindless errands and worry had sapped her of energy and initiative.

She sorted through the freezer for a microwave meal but found only the icy remains of a few desiccated dinners—nothing she could beg, pay or threaten her two boys to eat. She decided to run out to the nearby Boston Market. If she was going to be alone, worried sick about her husband, she at least would treat herself and the boys to a better-than-average fast-food meal.

She called into the family room that she would be back in a half hour. Their grunted acknowledgment told her they had no more idea whether she'd said she was going to the moon or joining the Marines.

As soon as Joan started the car, she slipped an old CD into the player and began singing softly to Nanci Griffith's "Time of Inconvenience." She loved Griffith's twangy, luscious east-Texas voice and the rich, mournful overtones. And something about that song spoke directly to Joan's sorrow. Griffith's pain was Joan's anguish too. Griffith's lyrics sang Joan's unspoken words. Somehow the magic of the song made Joan's feet tap and her heart hope.

Joan had always hated Noah's occasional travel, but she had never felt more alone than she did now. This afternoon's phone call had been the worst one of their marriage. He had made no apology or given her any hint of what was going on.

And he had called her babe.

She began to think about the rich, moist Boston Market creamed spinach. She knew the boys hated anything wet and green, but she decided she was going to eat what she wanted. She would salve the wounds of the day with white meat, green spinach, mounds of mashed potatoes, and the piece of chocolate cake she had hidden in the vegetable drawer since her sons' birthday party.

Noah might be having an affair, recklessly living the fast life, but she knew how to indulge her senses too. She knew how to throw a wild party for one. She would check out a weepy chick flick on DVD, pick up a People magazine, and escape after dinner to a hot bath. She would throw caution to the wind and indulge all her senses. And then, later—

I will not purge. I will not purge. The unbidden words came gurgling up from deep inside her. No one knew that she occasionally struggled with an old desire to rid herself of some inner demons by binging and purging.

When she was a junior in college, Joan had often gorged herself on junk food and then forced herself to throw up. She had always hated the acidic, unclean taste

*and felt humiliated by the violence of the act. And it had also brought her a deep
relief, a pleasure unlike any she had known in her rigid, angry home.*

*Binging and purging was a ritual that for some reason passed away when she
began to attend a Bible study on campus that year. When she confessed what she
called her "dirty habit" to a male campus leader, he had scrunched up his face and
told her talk to one of the female staff. Joan had never done so, but his response
had deepened her disgust for herself. But his repulsion had also seemed to help her
break the pattern over a period of months. Despite the occasional urges, she had
not made herself throw up for over fifteen years.*

Where did that thought come from? *she thought now.* What is my problem? I think about having a nice evening and somehow surviving this pain,
and then I ruin it with the thought of vomiting. How sick is that? *Joan popped
out the CD, and punched the button for a Christian station, and listened to praise
music for the rest of the trip to Boston Market.*

*When she got back to the car with her bags of food, a talk show had begun on
the radio:*

". . . is author and speaker Chuck Richburg, who has written the book Seven
Ways to Get Heaven Now. *Folks, I have been looking forward to this interview for
weeks. Chuck, your work gives us hope. Too many books tell us that life is hard.
Your book is a great antidote to despair. Welcome to the show."*

"Leonard, great to be with you. You are absolutely right. I wrote Seven Ways
to Get Heaven Now *to let Christians know that we are the victors, the winners of
life, and that God wants to give us the pleasures of heaven right now."*

*"Chuck, tell our listeners what they all are eager to hear. How can we claim
some of our eternal rewards?"*

*"I believe it is crucial for us to gratefully receive all that God has for us here on
earth. Think about a meal. If the cook prepares a sumptuous dinner but you don't
come to the table or pick up your fork, you will never enjoy what the cook has so
painstakingly prepared. That's an insult and a pity. We need to expect the Lord to
prepare a banquet for us each and every day—served at a table prepared for us in
the green pastures of his love."*

"Great word picture from Psalm 23, Chuck. Now, how do we get to the banquet?"

"Let's go through the seven promises God gives us in his Word. These promises tell us precisely what we need to do to make sure we sit at that great meal. Step number one is—"

Joan slammed her palm against the radio off button. She had heard enough about provision, pleasure, heavenly food and doing the "right thing" to secure God's favor. She had read the books. She had attended the seminars. And she was angry. She felt something godless and mean rising up in her heart. She wanted to swear— against whom she did not know, but she wanted to let someone in the universe know she was protesting what was said in the name of Christ.

She drove into the garage and grabbed the food for the kids. She didn't feel like praying. She didn't feel like eating, watching her video, reading her magazine, or even indulging in a warm bath. She felt sick, and if she could find a way to cleanse herself from the words she had heard in the car and the pain that seemed to buzz around her head, she would have been willing to purge. But there was little to be done but to set the table, fill the boys' plates with chicken and just enough spinach to gross them out, and then let them rip apart the defenseless bird.

Joan went into the study and found her Bible. She knew the psalm the men had been talking about, but she needed to see the words in print. She dropped the thick, leather-covered volume in her lap and flipped through until she found the Twenty-third Psalm. When she got to verse 4, she started to laugh:

Even when I walk
   through the darkest valley,
I will not be afraid,
   for you are close beside me.
Your rod and your staff
   protect and comfort me.

Amazing, *she thought.* Two great radio Bible teachers, and they left out this crucial verse. Comfort comes, but in the valley of death, not in the luxury of heaven. But what in the world is God's comfort when my life feels like it's dissolving, my husband is gone—maybe really gone—and I'm sick of being who I am? I'm sick of hurting, of seeing friends suffer. I'm just sick, sick, sick.

Tears, big, full-bodied tears, burst from some unseen dam that had held her heart in place. She gave in to the pleasure of sorrow, and her tears flowed down the river that so many saints before her had cut into the dry earth.

❦

The Idol: "Pleasure Will Satisfy Me"

For some people, pleasure means sex. For some it means food. Others seek the mindless escapism of television or the adrenaline rush of physically threatening risks. When any of these pleasurable pursuits turn into an all-consuming passion, it becomes an idol and, like any idol, it ultimately lets its worshipers down.

Whatever the pleasure, its effect is brief, and when it's over we often feel a deeper ache than before. Indeed, holding on to a good feeling is harder than holding on to the wind. But that doesn't stop most of us from trying.

Noah's real pleasure is work, but after a grueling and uncertain day, he turned from his fear and exhaustion to food, drink and a stimulating night on the town. Joan turned to music to soothe her fragmented heart. She also coped with her fear and pain by enjoying a special meal and indulging in a movie and a hot bath to escape from her fear and pain.

So what are we to think about Noah's flight from the day's battle? His culinary indulgence and imbibing of wine is clearly an effort to put the day behind him. And Joan's plans for the evening are clearly an attempt to take a break from consuming worry.

Were they wrong? Or is it all right for Christians to seek pleasure as a respite for weariness or pain?

Is God a Killjoy?

- If it tastes good, it will probably give you cancer.
- If it feels good, it must be immoral.
- If it's fun, it's probably dangerous.

- If it smells enticing, *it is* likely seductive.
- If it sounds pleasant, it is probably superficial.
- If it's pleasurable, it must not be biblical.

Many of us grew up with these warnings ringing in our ears from parents, teachers and the church. Christianity sometimes can seem to be the enemy of pleasure in general and especially of those *sensuous* pleasures that appeal to our sense of smell, touch, taste, sight and hearing. After all, we are interested in growing our spirits, not our bodies, which anchor us to this present world.

Some forms of pleasure can certainly be perverse. Joan, at one point in her life, found a kind of strange pleasure in binging and purging—a dangerous and unhealthy pursuit. It's not hard to think of other forms of sensual indulgence that promise pleasure but bring only heartache.

And yet the Bible is far from negative about pleasure itself, and many passages actually praise God for it. The psalmist writes,

> He makes grass grow for the cattle,
>   and plants for man to cultivate—
>   bringing forth food from the earth:
> wine that gladdens the heart of man,
>   oil to make his face shine,
>   and bread that sustains his heart. (Psalm 104:14-15 NIV)

"Wine to gladden the heart" implies a degree of joy brought through the chemical effects of the wine. There are a number of degrees of intoxication, and the word in this passage implies a slight buzz, a small but pleasant change of mood due to the wine. The psalm suggests this is not only all right with God, but part of his provision.

That's a radical notion for many Christians. Many will be offended by the psalmist's praise of God for providing wine, with its potential for dulling sorrow and invigorating pleasure. But it's right there in the Bible, along with many other passages that celebrate sensuous pleasure. We simply must reconsider our view of pleasure in the light of what the Bible clearly says.

Think back to the promise given to the people of God in the Old Testament time period. God promised to give his people a country of their own, a special land "flowing with milk and honey" (Exodus 3:8; 33:3; Deuteronomy 26:9). The image of milk and honey is intentionally sensuous. These thick, luscious liquids linger on the palate. They are rich symbols of blessing and enjoyment.

Or take the equally sensuous divine promise found in the chapters of Jeremiah often called the "Book of Consolation" (31—33). After describing the punishment that God's people would receive for their sins, Jeremiah gives them this promise from the Lord:

> The LORD has redeemed Israel
>> from those too strong for them.
> They will come home and sing songs of joy on the heights of
>> Jerusalem.
>> They will be radiant because of the LORD's good gifts—
> The abundant crops of grain, new wine, and olive oil,
>> and the healthy flocks and herds.
> Their life will be like a watered garden,
>> and all their sorrows will be gone. (Jeremiah 31:11-12)

God created us with senses and desires for a reason. He created a beautiful and enjoyable world for our pleasure. Our bodies are not a trap that we need to ignore or abuse to achieve spiritual enlightenment. That is a Buddhist concept, not a Christian one. The world is not a shadow that masks true reality. We are not souls imprisoned in flesh. The world is real, created by God for human enjoyment.

Pleasure heightens our senses. It increases our awareness. It lifts us above the routine and helps us survive adversity. Most important, it can point us toward God and move us to praise. It is truly a divine gift.

We can certainly understand this when we consider sexual intercourse, perhaps the most sensuous and pleasurable of all human experiences. Sexual intimacy arouses all the human senses. Sounds, smells, taste, sight and of course touch all come into play in lovemaking. The Song of Songs (or Song of Solomon), a biblical book that is also a passionate love poem, confirms this in the metaphors it employs to refer to the couple's love.

Throughout the Song of Songs, the description of the woman focuses on her physical beauty. It uses images of taste, reflecting the deep kisses the man places all over her body (Song of Songs 4:3, 11; 5:1). The man describes her breasts as twin fawns (4:5), an image of softness, anticipating his touch. Every conceivable sweet-smelling spice describes the garden, which is her body (4:13-15). Their conversation is the ecstatic sound that arouses them to climax.

God made us to enjoy bodily pleasure and blesses our enjoyment of sex, food, drink, beauty. But if all that is so, why do we find so little real pleasure in life? And why is it that the things we enjoy doing so often seem to lead to our harm?

The Problem of Pleasure

God created Adam and Eve with a capacity to relish life. He created a world that provided the opportunity for intense and satisfying sensuous pleasure. Yet the first humans weren't satisfied with the blessing that God had generously given them. They gave in to temptation, ate the one fruit they were supposed to avoid and got themselves thrown out of the Garden. Ever since, the experience of pleasure has been problematic, both a blessing and a curse.

Does it have to be that way? Is it possible for pleasure not only to nourish and momentarily satisfy but also to increase our hunger for what lies beyond the moment of satisfaction? We believe it can. But the pursuit of pleasure can also be a problem. The real danger is when pleasure satisfies without increasing a hunger for the God who made all pleasure.

Honest people will admit that life is a struggle—and the Teacher in the book of Ecclesiastes was hard-nosed in his honesty. After observing that people live most of their lives "frustrated, discouraged, and angry" (5:17), he goes on to encourage them to pursue some measure of relief through plea-surable experience:

> It is good and proper for a man to eat and drink, and to find satisfac-tion in his toilsome labor under the sun during the few days of life God has given him—for this is his lot. Moreover, when God gives any man wealth and possessions, and enables him to enjoy them, to accept his lot and be happy in his work—this is a gift of God. He seldom re-flects on the days of his life, because God keeps him occupied with gladness of heart. (5:18-20 NIV)

This passage is extremely subtle. Remember that the Teacher is giving this advice after he has concluded that life has no meaning. This passage, and the others like it are commonly referred to as *carpe diem* passages, referring to the Latin phrase meaning "seize the day." In contemporary phraseology, these passages say "Grab all the gusto you can."

We need to pay close attention to what the Teacher is saying here. The purpose of pleasure, he implies, is to keep us from thinking about our trou-bles. We can watch TV all evening and not give a thought to the fact that we have a horrible relationship with our children. We can take a vacation and sit on the beach to forget about our demeaning job back home. Plea-sure, in other words, serves as a kind of anesthetic to the soul. And that, implies the Teacher, is the best we can hope for in a world without meaning or ultimate purpose.

As I read the book of Ecclesiastes, I can't help but think that the Teacher himself was not one of the privileged few who can divert themselves through simple pleasure. His frustration and disappointment with the setbacks of life speak too loudly for me to think he includes himself among those who can drown their disappointment with a few drinks. Rather, I hear him speaking these words with both wistfulness and a measure of disdain. How can some-one live from party to party as if everything were fine in the world? he seems to be saying. And even if the world is just peachy keen, there is a little prob-lem called death that is going to take all the fun away.

With this latter point in mind, the Teacher gives his listeners some morbid advice:

Better to spend your time at funerals than at parties.
>After all, everyone dies—
>so the living should take this to heart.
Sorrow is better than laughter,
>for sadness has a refining influence on us.
A wise person thinks a lot about death,
>while a fool thinks only about having a good time. (7:2-4)

If this advice seems contradictory to his earlier advice about grabbing all the enjoyment we can, that's because it is! The Teacher is struggling under the sun, apart from God's revelation. Part of him would love to melt into the oblivion of pleasure, but he knows that to do so is to ignore reality. He's painfully aware that, apart from God, pleasure is just a momentary diversion before death.

Why then doesn't pleasure ultimately satisfy? Because it wasn't meant to. Pleasure was never intended to fill our deepest desires and needs, but to point us toward the One who can. When we turn to pleasure as a substitute for God, when it becomes an idol, we're setting ourselves up for problems.

Idolatry and Addiction

I love barbecue potato chips. If they are done just right, with the proper amount of flavoring, they taste so good going down. However, I am never satisfied with one chip or even a lunch-sized bag. I always want more. I know that eating too many will make me feel slightly ill and certainly guilty about my weight. But I am amazed how rarely that knowledge stops me eating chip after chip. The pleasure of one leads to a desire for the next.

And that's the problem with much of the pleasure we find under the sun. It never leads to complete satisfaction. It always leaves us wanting more. But recognizing the transience of pleasure rarely makes us give up on it. Instead, we tend to pursue pleasure all the more intensely, especially when we're feeling empty.

When life is hard, pleasure can be more than a diversion. It can easily become a need. We easily move from a properly moderate enjoyment of sensuous experience to a consuming desire for it.

Noah put in long, long hours as an analyst. His work on the Pearson project led him to challenge the conventional wisdom of the firm, and that put him into a make-or-break struggle with the top leadership and even the owners of the company. Noah was up against huge forces, including feelings fueled by a holocaust that had occurred nearly sixty years earlier. His reputation and his livelihood were on the line.

When he finished the meeting, he needed to be the team player by joining the group for dinner. His attempt at connecting with his wife by phone only made him feel worse, especially since he had not told her about the trip. Noah was in hot water both at work and home.

He went out to dinner with his associates to avoid offending them and to gather information that would direct his strategy for the next day. But he also went to dinner to escape the pressures the day had brought and his discomfort over his relationship with Joan. And it worked. The glorious meal, the free-flowing wine, and the convivial conversation transported him to the Novocain numbness that the Teacher recommends in the *carpe diem* passages.

Was Noah wrong to do this? Yes. He used legitimate pleasures to avoid facing his anger at Joan for her conversation in the car. Add to this the tension and fear about the next day's meeting, and it should be clear that Noah used pleasure to numb himself from his painful realities. Pleasure at that point was an anesthetic rather than a stimulus to consider God's goodness.

Pleasure is meant to prompt us to praise God. Whenever we use it to numb our souls, as the Teacher describes, to avoid facing our troubles, we usually end up overindulging to the point of oblivion. We overdo the pleasure to accomplish the desired end: escape.

A healthy enjoyment of pleasure has a boundary, an acknowledged limit that allows the heart to taste present goodness while also whetting the appetite for more. It enriches the heart and body while also, paradoxically, causing the heart to hunger, to ache for what no earthly pleasure can provide: a direct, consuming encounter with God.

Sadly, few people embrace pleasure for this purpose. Instead, they allow the pursuit of pleasure to lead them into idolatry and to addiction.

Consider the typical American couple. Both work hard all day, then spend the evening getting their kids to do their homework and finish their chores. At bedtime, they tuck in the kids, read them a short Bible passage, hear them say their prayers, and kiss them good night. Then, exhausted, the parents flop into bed, whip out the remote, and watch TV until they fall asleep—only to wake up in the morning and begin the routine again.

There's nothing inherently evil about this. Nor is it always wrong to escape the drudgery of a difficult world with some pleasant diversion. But we can slowly, unintentionally, mindlessly become dependent on those things that take us away from our problems and give us a shot of Novocain in the soul. We may soon find that what our soul yearns for more than anything else is not God or our family but HGTV or ESPN.

It may not be the television that does the trick. It may be other innocuous occupations like video games, reading, playing tennis, or sleeping. It may also be seriously damaging and dangerous pursuits like promiscuous sex, heavy drinking, illegal drugs or the like.

The tragedy, though, is that none of these sources of pleasure will ultimately satisfy us. Eventually we will have to turn off the TV to go to work. Eventually we have to come down from our high, and the drugs will eventually lose their effectiveness. The orgasm will end, followed by exhaustion and then ultimately the need for another sexual fix.

And then there is death. Death takes away all pleasure, evil and benign. If we live our lives for pleasure, we know that it will end once and for all with death. As the Teacher says, "The dead know nothing. They have no further reward, nor are they remembered. Whatever they did in their lifetime—loving, hating, envying—is all long gone. They no longer play a part in anything here on earth" (Ecclesiastes 9:5-6).

If we pursue pleasure for its own sake, it will always eventually disappoint. If we live our lives for those things that tingle our senses or numb our feelings, we will become entrapped in our devotion to them. Eventually they will not only will deny us the joy we want, but also, ultimately, bring us pain.

The Pitfall of Boredom

The Old Testament tells us that, in early days, many of God's children were seduced to worship the false gods of other civilizations. Biblical and archaeological texts tell us that much of the appeal of this worship came from its promise of sensual pleasure—because worship of false gods often involved activities that were not permissible to the Israelites.

We see this at the time Aaron and the people turned against God in the wilderness and worshiped the golden calf. They had waited more than a month at the base of Mt. Sinai while Moses spoke with God on the mountain. Eventually they grew restless and decided to fashion an idol to worship.

Remember the conversation between Moses and Joshua as they returned to the camp after receiving the Ten Commandments?

When Joshua heard the boisterous noise of the people shouting below them, he exclaimed to Moses, "It sounds like war in the camp!" But Moses replied, "No, it's not a shout of victory nor the wailing of defeat. I hear the sound of a celebration" (Exodus 32:17-18).

What they were hearing was the aftermath of the idol's construction. The people "celebrated with feasting and drinking, and they indulged in pagan revelry" (v. 6)—which likely included sexual relations among the worshipers, a common aspect of the worship of fertility gods in the ancient Near East.

The point is that the Israelites were tempted by activities that promised to take them out of their everyday humdrum existence. We, too, can be lured by experiences that give our humdrum worlds a shot of excitement. When we're bored, the pursuit of even illicit pleasure has a stronger pull on us.

Boredom arises in the context of a lack of purpose and passion. If we feel no interest in the world around us and don't know where we're going, we feel empty and restless. And that restlessness can propel us into desperate, unwise attempts at finding pleasure.

Boredom is usually thought to accompany a lack of activity, but we can be bored just as easily when we are busy. Many, many people hate their work because they find it boring. This is just as true of people who work in high-powered professional jobs as it is of those who work routine manual jobs. Boredom arises when people feel no passion or desire, no interest in the activity with which they are involved.

Boredom is the younger sibling of sadness and depression. If felt intensely and for a long enough period of time, it can grow to the proportions of despair—or worse. According to University of Virginia professor Patricia Spacks's intriguing study of boredom as a literary and psychological category, boredom can even mask an underlying rebellion and aggression. She recounts the report of a young person who committed a random murder, justifying his act with the casual comment, "I was bored."

That's an extreme example. But even less dangerous attempts at alleviating boredom with excesses of pleasure can sabotage a well-rounded and enjoyable life.

I remember a long period in my childhood when I battled with loneliness. I had just moved to Columbus, Ohio, from New Jersey. I had no real friends to speak of, but I found solace in reading. Books were (and still are) my "drug of choice." Through a good book, I could escape the tedium of routine and enter a much more exciting world. The trouble was, reading also kept me from doing what I needed to connect with others.

My mother would beg me to go out and play with the neighbor children. I really wanted to do that, but I was too frightened at the possibility of rejection. I remember going out the door as if to play and then sneaking back into the house through another door. I would quietly go upstairs into my rather spacious closet. Closing the door and turning on a flashlight, I would spend the morning with my nose in a book.

I read the entire Tom Swift series and more in that closet. But eventually I tired of Tom, and I couldn't make the time pass so quickly. I remember looking at the clock and feeling disappointment that it was only midafternoon. Those minutes and hours before a decent TV show came on (another escape from the empty hours) seemed an eternity to me. It wasn't until I finally ventured into the neighborhood and made some friends that my new life really began in that place.

Nothing New Under the Sun

Boredom is a relatively common part of our experience because our world can a boring place—or at least that's the view of the Teacher. The book of Ecclesiastes opens with a depressing—but familiar—picture of a relentlessly repetitive existence.

> Generations come and generations go, but the earth never changes. The sun rises and the sun sets, then hurries around to rise again. The wind blows south, and then turns north. Around and around it goes, blowing in circles. Rivers run into the sea, but the sea is never full. Then the water returns again to the rivers and flows out again to the sea. Everything is wearisome beyond description. No matter how much we see, we are never satisfied. No matter how much we hear, we are not content. History merely repeats itself. It has all been done before. Nothing under the sun is truly new. Sometimes people say, "Here is something new!" But actually it is old; nothing is ever truly new. (1:4-9)

Today I am writing on my back porch, where I can take a moment to look up at the beautiful fall foliage in my backyard. While the colors are striking, I am not surprised by them. I have seen the same scene every fall for the past sixteen years that I have lived here. I drive on the same roads most days, back and forth from the seminary, and when I go on a trip to a new location, the planes, hotels and scenery are pretty much the same everywhere. The longer we live, the more callous we become because these "new" experiences are really not so new.

Even our actions are not new. It is a common ploy of ministers and politicians to tell us that our society has never sunk so low. As a student of history, I can only agree with the Teacher: "Do not say, 'Why were the old days better than these?' For it is not wise to ask such questions" (7:10 NIV).

Why isn't this question a wise one? Because everyone but the greatest fool knows that the past was as bad as the present and the future.

In Search of a Good Feeling

There truly is nothing new under the sun, so boredom is an inescapable experience. And people often pursue pleasure in harmful and destructive ways just to escape the humdrum routine. They think this life is all there is, so they feel compelled to try to enjoy every second of it. Since pleasure is a false god, however, tantalizing but never fulfilling us, they find themselves sucked into an obsessive pursuit of a good feeling. Eventually they become too numb to feel anything at all.

The movie *The People vs. Larry Flynt,* a commentary on the decadence in our society, focuses on the life of the pornographer who founded *Hustler* magazine. But it also portrays the sad life of his wife, who allowed nothing to stand in the way of a good feeling. As the movie progresses, she moves from being a shocking woman to a pathetic creature, a slave to her pursuit of pleasure. To achieve her end, she engages in bizarre sexual behavior and also becomes a serious drug addict. Sex becomes so ordinary to her that it no longer provides any satisfaction. She changes from a young and vibrant woman to a haggard person obsessed only with pursuing her next high. She eventually contracts AIDS, and her body and mind slowly follow her soul in its deterioration.

It is hard for many people to identify with someone like Flynt's wife. But even God-fearing people can find themselves caught up in an obsessive and futile pursuit of pleasure.

Why? Because they come to God with a false understanding: they think they aren't supposed to suffer.

Jesus promises us abundant life now and an eternity with him. But he never guarantees a constant run of good feelings. And if we come to him expecting nonstop happiness and excitement, we face disappointment, because we inevitably find our struggles aren't over. We suffer as a result of our own sin and the sin of others. We suffer pain and, yes, boredom in our daily lives. Where is the joy? Where is the abundant life? Where are those good feelings we expected?

No wonder we find ourselves chasing after pleasure. It's because we haven't understood what God can do with our honest pain.

Joy in the Midst of Suffering

Our experience confirms that the Teacher was right when he said that joy under the sun is fleeting and does not fulfill us. Scripture teaches that life is a struggle and suffering is inevitable in this fallen world. According to Paul, we "suffer now" because "all creation was subjected to God's curse" (Romans 8:18, 20). But Scripture also makes it clear that, if we trust God, suffering can make us stronger people and draw us closer to him (1 Peter 5:10). And coming to him with our pain rather than numbing ourselves with pleasure is the secret to finding true joy.

This reality may not have been in Joan's mind when she went to pick up dinner. But when she listened to the wistful, sorrowful Nanci Griffith song, she sang along quietly, letting the pain of her day with Erin, her sadness over Jessie's hard life, the confusion of the past weeks and the turmoil of her phone call with Noah express itself through the music.

Joan did not flee sorrow. She sang along with it. But she also decided to enjoy a good meal and an escape from the normal routine of making a meal for her kids. Her plan for a nice bath, a new magazine and a video seems less of a flight from reality than an acknowledgment that she could do little about her situation except strengthen herself to stay in the battle.

Was this a conscious, well-thought-through plan? No. Joan was hurt, angry and confused, casting around blindly for some way to make herself feel better. Notice, however, what Joan did *not* do. Though tempted, she did not succumb to her old pattern of binging and purging. She did not watch more TV. She made plans to indulge in relatively harmless pleasures—healthy food, a magazine and a well-loved movie.

But God had other plans for Joan that night. Her memory of old patterns of finding relief in the midst of pain compelled her to turn on the radio. And though the Christian talk show she listened to was so unreal that it infuriated her, the passionate anger it aroused opened her heart to honest sorrow . . . and the possibility of real healing for her hurt.

For Joan the pursuit of legitimate pleasure brought comfort. Comfort brought relief, but it brought even deeper desire. Her desire for more brought back memories of how she used to kill her heart's desire when it unnerved her, and God used that memory to send her fleeing to the radio. That flight brought a fight, and the fight brought her back to the only One who can offer dependable comfort and pleasure: Jesus, the One who suffered ultimate pain for our pleasure.

To live confident, happy lives, we must understand the paradox that true joy comes in the midst of suffering. We find pleasure not by denying the pain of life but in facing it. "Because of our faith, Christ has brought us into this place of undeserved privilege where we now stand, and we confidently and joyfully look forward to sharing God's glory. We can rejoice, too, when we run into problems and trials, for we know that they help us develop endurance" (Romans 5:2-3). Or, as 2 Corinthians so beautifully puts it: "Our hearts ache, but we always have joy" (6:10).

Joy in the midst of suffering! That sounds wonderful, but what does it really mean? Does it mean that we feel happy, not sad, when we discover we have terminal cancer or when our child is arrested? Nothing could be further from the truth.

We can rejoice in the midst of our present sufferings because we know with an absolute certainty that this life is not the end of our story. The author of the book of Hebrews encourages his fellow Christians when he says to them, "You suffered along with those who were thrown into jail, and when all you owned was taken from you, you accepted it with joy. You knew there were better things waiting for you that will last forever" (Hebrews 10:34).

We know, after all, that we will once again return to the Garden (Revelation 22). In fact, we'll experience something even better. We will live forever in the presence of God, where every tear will be wiped away (21:4). Like the psalmist in Psalm 73, we know that though the ungodly seem happier on the surface than we are now, God will lead us "to a glorious destiny" (v. 24).

Jesus himself is our model, and we follow in his glorious path. We share in Christ's sufferings when we experience disappointment and trouble. But Jesus' death was not the end of his story. No, he was brought into his Father's presence, where he rules over the universe. In the same way, our complete fulfillment will take place in the future, and that knowledge can sustain us in the present.

Pleasure in the Present

Am I saying that Christianity is nothing but "pie in the sky by and by"? Absolutely not. It is true that complete fulfillment will come only in heaven, but God in his grace gives us glimpses of what is to come.

We get a taste of the pleasures of heaven now, and that taste often comes through sensuous pleasure. The enjoyment of a delicious meal, the sound of a powerful symphony, the aroma of a lily, the caress of a loved one—these and other experiences have the power to release us from the grip of our present turmoil and cause us consider the incomprehensible joys that lie ahead of us. They sustain us as we live in a trouble-filled world.

These pleasures are God-given gifts for our enjoyment. While we cannot find our ultimate meaning in this world, we must not feel guilt as we enjoy these pleasures. We must remember that when we delight in pleasure, God is pleased. He has, after all, built our bodies with intense nerve endings suited to the stimulation of the senses. Sitting down to a sumptuous meal or experiencing the ecstasy of sexual intercourse with our spouse should cause us to praise our Creator and look forward to the heavenly joys to which these pleasures point us.

Pleasure Above the Sun

Under the sun, pleasure frustrates. It can be wonderful, but it doesn't last long under the sun, and ultimately it lets us down. And as long as we think that all we have is the present life, the transience of pleasure can lead to obsessive or even addictive pursuit, the excessive need to experience the feeling again. We may be driven to illicit desire for unhealthy forms of pleasure. And we will tend to seek only pleasure and avoid pain at all costs.

If we fear God, however, we will recognize that true pleasure is that which anticipates the glory to come. However—and this is an important distinction—that does not mean that all legitimate pleasure is abstract, intellectual, or spiritual. Indeed, sensuous pleasure is at the heart of God. He built us with the dense nerve endings that lead to intense sensual desire. He wants us to enjoy the world he made . . . but in the right context.

So savor a delicious meal, not just for itself, but as a gift from God. Be carried away by powerful music as an anticipation of the music of heaven. Be enticed by the smell of the sea, the scent of a flower. Be seduced by the caresses and kisses of your spouse. Enjoy these moments of bliss as God's gift that opens a brief glimpse of the utter ecstasy to come when we live in God's glorious presence.

Taking a Closer Look

Reread Ecclesiastes 1:4-10.

1. Verses 5-7 describe three natural phenomena that go around in circles. What are they? Does your life sometimes feel like it is going around in circles? Give examples.

2. Verse 10 asks, "What can you point to that is truly new?" Can you think of anything? In what way is it new?

How Do We Chase After Pleasure?

1. Be honest with yourself. What do you enjoy doing more than anything else? If you had a completely free day, all the money in the world, and no sense of guilt, how would you spend that day?

2. Does the search for pleasure ever consume you? Do you avoid pleasure?

Would you consider yourself an addictive person? How would others characterize you?

3. Imagine your most enjoyable day, doing exactly what you want to do for fun and relaxation. After that day, do you see yourself thanking God? Trying to forget that God knows what you've done? Not even giving God a thought? Why or why not?

4. What sensual pleasures do you enjoy in life?

5. Would you characterize the pleasure you experience as a gift from God or an idol that enslaves? If the latter, how do you break the bondage?

6. How can you enjoy life in the midst of disappointment and even pain?

7. What do the feelings of joy you experience in the present teach you about heaven?

8. What Scripture passages help you understand God's joy when we feel pleasure?

5

CHASING AFTER WISDOM

"Knowledge Will Put Me on Top"

Noah woke to the sound of a phone ringing somewhere in the room. He knew he heard it, but he couldn't reach for it. He felt pinned to the bed.

The next thing Noah became aware of was his mouth. It felt dry, thick. Even if he could find the phone, he was pretty sure he couldn't speak. The phone kept ringing as he gradually became aware of where he was and what he had to do. He had to get up and prepare either to be fired or to be promoted for his report on the Pearson stock.

The ringing finally stopped. Noah plodded to the shower without looking at the mirror. He knew that looking would only sicken him more. Why did I drink so much? I didn't think it was that much, but maybe it was combination of the food and the wine—actually a lot of wine. I hope I didn't say anything I shouldn't have.

His mind tried in vain to reconstruct the conversation at the Blue Note. He could not even recall the taxi ride home. No matter. Nothing he said last night could influence the Andrajian brothers' decision. It all hinged on whether they were willing to make a change.

Brothers Consolidated had a long history of selling stocks short and had made a great deal of money through the formula they used to determine when to buy and sell. In one major stock evaluation report, Noah had effectively thrown that formula into the dumpster and challenged the way the firm did business. And no one really believed the brothers would permit an upstart analyst from Chicago to take the firm down an utterly different path.

Conventional wisdom could not have been more wrong.

When Noah reached the thirty-eighth floor, sweat already dampened his starched white collar. A couple of secretaries greeted him as he made his way to the conference room, but the executives gathered there barely acknowledged his arrival. He was clearly marked as the sacrificial offering, and no one wanted to be mistaken as his confidant. Noah willed himself to appear calm as he found a chair and stowed his briefcase. His mouth still felt like it was full of cotton.

The Andrajian brothers entered the room, and the meeting began.

Stephen Andrajian, the younger brother, was clearly not one for small talk. He launched right in to the matter at hand. "Gentlemen, we have run a tight and competitive organization for many years. We have nothing to be ashamed of, and we are proud of the work you have all done. But the market is changing. Business is changing. We must change. We have reviewed the work of Mr. Noah Adamson, and we consider his insight and knowledge of the Pearson account to be a useful paradigm for evaluation and decision making on all our accounts."

Sam Andrajian, the older brother, looked at Noah and smiled. "Noah, I know that many people in this room doubted your work. They probably also assumed your employment in this firm would soon be finished. Nothing could be further from the truth. We would like you to consider taking the position of senior vice president of analysis, working from Chicago, of course, but advising and monitoring all the other analysts. We would like to know in several days if this would be acceptable to you. Of course, we plan to increase your income proportionate to the weight of the position."

James McKenna and his staff of five paled and barely breathed as Sam spoke. It was a clear palace coup, and the senior analyst obviously felt the blade suspended over his neck.

The brothers did not wait for anyone to speak. They stood and walked out. Sam Andrajian walked by Noah, laid a meaty hand on his shoulder, and squeezed it. "Good job, son."

The room seemed to lose air. The men stared straight ahead, and no one said a word. Finally, Noah rose. He gathered up his briefcase. No one moved. Before Noah made it to the door, one of the junior men finally spoke. "Nice job. I just look forward to working with you."

Noah walked out of the room with his head swirling. He simply could not fathom what just happened. He walked to the elevator and didn't know whether to dance or to maintain his professional cool. He quickly calculated that his salary would triple and that his power would grow well beyond that of his bosses in the Chicago office. In fact, Noah slowly realized, he had just become their boss, at least in matters that affected their lives on the most basic level: what they bought and sold, and therefore how much they earned.

A gust of wind hit him squarely in the face when he walked out the door and onto Fifty-fourth Street. His senses were alive, and the air felt almost abrasive. Checking his watch, he noticed he had five hours before his flight to Chicago was due to leave. He decided to take a walk. Holding his head high, he affected the swagger of a financial Brahmin.

Noah walked briskly as the wind whipped through the concrete canyons. He had not remembered to take along his trench coat, but he barely noticed the deepening chill.

He stopped at the window of a three-story bookstore. One of the books in the window promised financial security in a year's time. "Funny," he muttered to no one in particular, "I just achieved that in about ten minutes."

Noah thought back to the years and years of reading, the fine professors he studied with in graduate school, the lengthy conversations with the few who had encouraged him to pursue the risky world of stocks, and he chuckled, "No, it has been more like fifteen years that allowed those ten minutes to happen." He shuddered as he thought of the many hours he had spent in apparently purposeless study, review and conversation. The chill of the wind drove him into the bookstore.

As soon as Noah walked into the warmth of the bookstore, his queasiness returned. He dismissed it as the lingering effect of an indulgent night. He walked to the section that best fit his interests: business. The financial gurus beckoned to him as soon as he walked to their aisle. The glossy covers of the business books often pictured their authors: tan, confident, relaxed and unashamedly rich.

Noah lifted a few books from the shelf and settled into a comfortable chair to skim their contents.

The first book promised to lead readers into grand sums of money through real estate. The second book promised a calamity that would make gold necessary for backing up near-useless paper. The third promised an investment strategy that would net readers a guaranteed 12 percent return. Noah laughed out loud at the outlandish promises and dumped all three books on the floor. The bookstore hired people to put the books away; he didn't want them to lose their job.

As he left his chair, Noah walked past the psychology section. He picked up a few books and noticed almost identical claims—just with different focus. Depressed? This book will make you well in ten weeks. Divorced? You can find the love you deserve without all the hassle.

He seldom checked out the religion section of a bookstore, but now he felt the tug to explore what was on that shelf. He moved past the books that taught New Age chanting and channeling and the empowerment spirituality that offered readers the opportunity to become gods or goddesses. He finally found a few books that seemed to be based on the Bible. He walked back to his comfortable seat, scanned the dust jacket and the first few pages of one of them—and laughed again. The formula that governed the religious books was the same he had seen in the business and the psychology books.

Each book made promises he knew it could not fulfill; if it did, it went further than claims found in the Bible. Each book spoke in dignified tones but sounded the same shrill message. Follow these four steps (or seven steps, or twelve steps)— easily understood, somewhat demanding, but really quite simple to fulfill—and you, too, can have the world as you want it.

These books are no different from the others. What a game. It's the same sales job, no different from selling soap, fast cars or even soft porn. *Noah thought about the men sitting around the conference table. They had made the same mistake. They had gone for the conventional wisdom and fallen victim to the herd mentality.*

Noah's hands tightened around the book as he realized once more that he had just won. He had won because he had dared to break the mold and challenge the system. He had stepped outside the rut, and though he could have crashed and burned in one fiery moment, he had not bailed out. He had won.

⚶

Noah checked his watch. His brief detour into the bookstore had eaten up only another half hour. He had plenty of time to return to the hotel, check out and take a cab back to La Guardia.

He headed back up Fifty-fourth Street toward the hotel. It was midmorning, and the streets were relatively empty. His pace quickened as a cold shiver ran down his back. The wind seemed to have sharpened, and his suit coat couldn't keep the chill at bay.

Noah strode along, feeling like a gunslinger who had finished off the bad guys and was walking to collect his well-deserved reward. As he walked, his eyes fell on an older couple a half block ahead of him. They moved steadily, but age and something else he could not describe made their pace much slower than his. The woman appeared to be about seventy. Her hair was wrapped in a rain bonnet, and her feet sported galoshes that reminded him of boots girls wore when he was in fifth grade. Noah chuckled at her preparations for rain. It had been the driest fall in New York in years, and there was no prospect of precipitation.

As odd as the couple appeared, they were endearing even from forty yards behind. The woman's arm was linked around the man's left arm. His right hand gently touched her arm. It was clear she was the slower of the two, but he paced himself to her stride and mirrored her posture. His white head in its Winston hat was bent at about the same degree as her shoulders.

Noah sped up to get closer to them. Once he got within ten feet, he slowed down to keep a respectful distance. They were obviously Jewish; Noah saw prayer-shawl cords hanging underneath the man's coat. Close enough to hear them talk, he also noticed their accents, which he guessed were Eastern European. Noah was intrigued by their lively chatter, which lightly cloaked their tender regard for each other.

Noah loved New York for moments like this. He smiled and moved a little closer, just as he felt a surge of acidity in his mouth and deeper in his throat. His whole chest felt the seismic presence of heartburn. Noah was irritated that he had no antacid in his briefcase. He remarked out loud: "If I had talked to Joan before I left, she would have reminded me to—"

He stopped in midsentence. "Joan! I can't believe I haven't called her." He looked to heaven. "What was I thinking? I'm a mess."

Noah pulled out his cell phone, flipped it open, and snorted in frustration. The battery was dead again. He picked up his pace. He had to call Joan before he got on the plane—in part to let her know the great news, but mostly to apologize for the way he had been treating her.

He hurried past the couple he had been watching from a distance and turned quickly down an alley that he thought might save him a few minutes. He walked by the trash bins that blocked sight from the main street and wondered silently, I hope this is safe.

A kid in baggy pants leaned against a doorway. Noah passed him without speaking, then quickened his pace when he realized the kid had stepped out into the alleyway. A moment later he looked straight ahead and saw another kid come out from behind another trash bin, boxing him in. Noah willed himself to keep moving forward, acting confident.

The kid's hands grabbed him so quickly that at first he thought he had snagged his jacket, but then he was whirled against the wall and his head hit with a thud. One kid said, "Yell and you're dead. Gimme your wallet—and keep your eyes down."

The violent ballet had happened so swiftly that Noah forgot where he had put his wallet. He dug into his coat pocket and couldn't locate the familiar bulge. One of the kids grabbed his briefcase and emptied it on the ground. Papers flew down the alley.

Noah fumbled and stuck his hand into his pants pocket. He found a wad of bills, a credit card and the dead cell phone, but no wallet. He handed over the loot, but it was not enough for his muggers.

"Give us more, or you're dead meat." The kid behind him slammed Noah's head against the wall again. Then he felt the sharp edge of a knife slice through his shirt and graze his stomach.

"I don't have my wallet with me. It's in my hotel room. I just gave you all I've got. I don't have anything else—just the briefcase. But it's worth five hundred bucks. Take it. Just don't hurt me."

The kid drew his face to Noah's and began to laugh. His eyes were empty and almost uncomprehending; he was obviously on something. "He say he don't want me to hurt him. Well, I'm gonna—"

Noah shuddered, aware that one false movement or errant word might be his last. He cast his eyes left and then right, looking for some way to protect himself. And there, standing less than ten feet away, he saw the old man and woman he had just passed.

His surprise must have showed. Both boys turned quickly—and were met by a torrent of broken English.

"Look at you," the woman said sharply. "What you doing? What you doing to this goy. Hooligans. Vilda chaya. What you think he is, a schlemiel? You wanna piece of my mind? I'll tell your sisters and your mother that you're shtunk and up to no good. Now leave him alone and vamoose."

The old man stood by his wife with his hand on her shoulder and glared at the two boys. Noah would never be sure if the boys were simply unwilling to kill three people or if the woman's scolding so bewildered them that they decided to take the money and run. Whatever the reason, the knife disappeared back into the kid's coat as the boys grabbed the briefcase and sprinted away.

Noah couldn't make himself move or speak. He just stood there plastered against the wall.

The woman spoke more quietly. "Ask the man, Jakob, if he is hurt."

Noah managed to peel himself from the wall. He was still breathing hard. "I'm . . . I'm okay. But I wouldn't have been if you hadn't showed up."

The old man winked at his wife. "Rosie, if you want to know how he is, you ask him."

She smiled at Noah. "We've not been properly introduced, and my husband should be the one to make the introduction. I apologize for his rudeness, Mister—"

"Adamson. I'm Noah Adamson, and I'm utterly in your debt. How did you know I was in trouble?"

Jakob leaned over to pick up the few papers that had not blown away. "When my Rosie saw you turn down the alley, she said we needed to follow you. And I learned a long time ago not to stand in my wife's way when she has her mind made up."

"Those boys are always lurking around the neighborhood," his wife added. "They're usually up to no good."

"I certainly appreciate it." Noah numbly accepted the papers from Jakob. Some separate part of him noticed that the old man had salvaged his pocket calendar, a promotional brochure for Brothers Consolidated and a Starbucks receipt. "But you could have been killed."

Rosie laughed. "How can you kill a woman who's been through the Holocaust? How can you kill a woman who has cancer and is not afraid to die? Young man, you can only scare someone if they're foolish enough to think their life is their own. Me, I'm too old to worry and too happy with life to fear death."

"Well, I can't thank you enough." Noah felt tears begin to trickle down his face as a wave of fear finally seeped through his shock. He had almost died, and an old woman had yanked him out of the grave.

This woman.

He felt her quiet hand on his shoulder as he held his shaking head into his hands and sobbed, "What have I done to my wife?"

ॐ

An hour later, Noah slumped in the seat as the taxi hurtled through the congested streets toward LaGuardia. He leaned his head against the cool window as he tried to sort out images swirling through his mind.

He had been too stunned to articulate his feelings to Jakob and Rosie. He'd almost forgotten to get their address and phone number. But now, as he thought about what had happened, he realized a polite letter or a phone call would never do. He wanted to look into their faces and somehow do what he never had done with any human being. He wanted to thank them from the bottom of his heart just for existing.

He still hadn't been able to call Joan. By the time he made it back to the hotel, he had barely had time to pack, check out and hail the cab. Now he was in danger of missing his flight.

He dashed down the congested aisle to reach the plane door moments before it closed. He slumped in his first-class seat and let the flight attendant serve him a plastic glass of Scotch to calm the adrenaline that still surged through his veins. Then and only then did he feel the pounding of his head and the throb of the cut on his stomach. He made his way to the restroom, unbuttoned his shirt, and inspected the blue web of broken vessels and the red blob of coagulating blood.

A flight attendant knocked on the door to tell him he was holding up the plane's departure. He didn't care. She could have screamed in his face, and he would not have hurried a second faster.

Slowly he rebuttoned his stained shirt and peered at his face in the mirror. He had to know what he looked like—to discover what it was he had lost and never knew he possessed. His aging face looked back at him, pale and tired and lonely, but a strange flame shone in his eyes. It was a different from the spark he often saw before he made a big presentation or sparred with a colleague or jumped into unknown financial waters to wrest clarity from chaos. It was something he had never noticed before.

He looked like a man who had a soul.

The trip home was uneventful. Noah checked his rescued pocket calendar before landing and was stunned to realize that the Bible study was scheduled to meet at his home that night. He had forgotten all about the evening in the wash of the last few days. But now he realized he was thrilled. Even if the study were held at the shrine of Elvis and his car had to be impounded, he still wouldn't have missed that meeting.

By the time Noah got off the plane, he could barely walk. Each step was labored, his bloodstained shirt was sticking to his ribs, and he noticed his pants were torn and streaked with dirt.

He chuckled and smiled at the passing glances that indicated he was a spectacle.

❦

As each person arrived at the Bible study, Joan offered an flustered apology about Noah's absence. She had been praying all day, begging God for wisdom, feeling anything but wise. She had dialed Noah's cell number at least twenty times and gotten his voice mail. His assistant hadn't heard from him. Joan had no idea when he would be home . . . or if he was even alive.

Jack herded everyone into the family room and directed them to sit. "Joan, it is obvious you are in pain, and we don't want to intrude. But we also don't want to ignore what you've been going through. What do you need from us?"

Joan flushed as Jessie slid over and put an arm around her shoulder. She appreciated the warm concern she saw on every face, but she honestly didn't know what to say. "I think I'd—"

She froze in midsentence as she heard the sound of the garage door going up. Everyone else had frozen too. They waited for what seemed like an interminable period of time before Noah opened the side door, crossed the kitchen, and entered the family room where the Bible study group waited. He stood in the opening between the kitchen and family room, trench coat in one hand and his carry-on in the other. His clothes were dirty and disheveled, his face was tired. No one had ever seen Noah so soiled by life—or so radiant.

Joan slowly approached Noah as if a tow rope were drawing her up a steep incline. Noah dropped both his coat and bag, hobbled toward to his wife, and wrapped his arms around her. No words came. No tears flowed. He just stood there shaking, apparently unable to let go.

She slid her arms around him and guided him to her chair. Noah sat down meekly.

"Ah . . . maybe we should leave," Jack said. "It's obvious something has happened. Maybe it's better for you two to talk first without us here."

Joan opened her mouth to answer, but Noah held up his hand. "The last few days—actually the last six hours—are more than I can describe, but I want you to stay for a few minutes and let me tell you what I have gone through. Then—you're right. I have so many things to say to Joan, and at least for now, it's better for me to say them just to her."

Jack sat forward. "Are you in pain, Noah?"

"Actually, I am. I could use some Advil if anyone has some."

Joan jumped up and within a minute was back with water and three pills.

"Thanks, honey." Joan flinched. Another unfamiliar endearment—although this time he sounded sincere.

Jack gulped the pills and water, handed the glass back to Joan, and began. "On the way home," he said, "I got a Bible from the back of the plane and read through the first chapter of Ecclesiastes again. It was talking about the difference between wisdom and foolishness. And it basically said that wisdom isn't any different from any other endeavor. Because the more I know, the more wisdom I gain, the more sorrow I feel."

He looked over at Jack. "That's not an exact quote. And I don't know if I really get it all yet. But it's basically saying that knowledge and wisdom make things worse, not better, right?"

Jack nodded, and Noah continued. "I don't know how to tell you what I've been through the last few weeks. For one, I've been in this furious battle to change the direction of the company I work for. And today I won that war—not the battle, but the whole war. I was promoted to senior vice president of analysis for the entire firm. It's is an incredible honor. But I'm ashamed of what it took for me to get there. I've been so consumed with this war that I have neglected my wife, my boys and all of you too."

Noah gazed around at the intent, expectant faces. Joan kept her eyes riveted to the floor.

"But the success I achieved today was almost lost forever. I was almost lost." Now Joan's face frantically turned toward him.

"I almost died today." Noah's body began to shake again. He covered his face with his hands and let the tears stream unimpeded down his cheeks.

Joan hesitated. Then she stood and threw her arms around him, holding on tight. Jack instinctively bowed his head. Marcia followed, and soon the whole group was praying silently. When Noah's tears subsided after many minutes, Jack asked if he could pray for Noah and Joan.

Noah looked straight at him. "Jack, I have never needed someone to pray for me more than I do now." Jack rose, and without a word the group stood and surrounded the red-eyed Noah and silent Joan.

"Father, we are privileged beyond words to be part of this moment with two people we love. Beyond all words, we thank you for preserving Noah's life. We don't know the details. We know only that you were directly and intimately involved in plucking him from death. Whatever your purpose in this event, we ask that you *use it to further save his heart and win it for you. I ask that you would take his gratitude and use it to deepen his love for you, for his wife, for the path you have set for him from eternity. And Father, we pray that Noah will not try to figure out too soon what you are doing in his life. Keep him from his tendency to try to manage his life and figure out the principles you want him to learn. Give him instead a profound taste of your love."*

Jack said amen and stepped back while a few others prayed. After a few moments, they all returned to their seats—except for Joan, who sank down at his feet and leaned against his leg.

Noah looked at each person, feeling he had awakened from a dream. He saw tears in the eyes of many. He could not discount their love. He finally turned to Joan. "I don't know what to say. You know I haven't put a lot of energy into our relationship. To be honest, I've never really wanted to know you or the kids. And you probably know that too, but I didn't. If I had been wiser, I would've seen you were suffering, and I would've done something to change the direction of our world. But I didn't. And I don't have any excuse."

He reached down to take her hand. "I've spent my whole life learning and knowing more than anyone else in my field. And today it took me to both the height of my career . . . and almost to the end of my life."

"But what happened?" she whispered.

"It took me by surprise," he said. "I was just walking along, not really thinking, all full of pride and excitement about the job. And then . . . I walked into a mugging. I wasn't paying attention, and I walked right into it. They had a knife; they were going to kill me. But then this angel—a plump Jewish angel with a thick Eastern accent—stepped in and saved me."

Joan looked confused. "You mean—"

Noah smiled. "I can't tell you why, but for a couple blocks I had followed this old woman and her husband, thinking how great it was that they were in love. They could barely hobble along, but there was more passion and tenderness in the way they touched than you and I have ever had. But it's not your fault; it's . . ."

Noah closed his eyes as the tears flowed again. This time no one moved. They just waited for Noah to continue. "It's my fault," he finally managed. "I haven't *wanted to see what kind of man I was to my family—to you, Joan."*

He looked into his wife's gentle eyes. He shook his head. *"I thought I was so smart. How could I have been so stupid?"*

𝒟

The Idol: "Knowledge Ought to Put Me on Top"

The smarter we are, the easier it is to navigate life—or that's what we usually assume. We stand in awe of the high school valedictorian, the molecular scientist, the thirteen-year-old who graduates from MIT. We root for movie heroes who use their ingenuity to get themselves out of life-threatening jams, and we marvel when our favorite televised crime-scene crew apply their knowledge of trace evidence and DNA to solve the most arcane crimes.

Most of us want to be smarter because we want an edge in a world driven by information. As we see with Noah, knowledge is gold, and access to it is like having a pirate's map.

Noah's superior knowledge brought him success because he was willing to stand outside the stream of conventional wisdom. In fact, his practical knowledge of the ways of the world caused him to look with appropriate suspicion at what several self-help books offered. What is marketed as wisdom is often an illusion of mastery that disappears in thin air when reality dawns.

The stacks of self-help books that promised Noah control and power did not allure him; they sickened him. But his disgust at their superficial solutions and hollow promises did not compel him to challenge the basis of his own knowledge or what he did with it. It allowed him only to stand aside from the marketing pitches and feel superior. It would take another of God's intrusions into his life to compel him to reconsider what he "knew."

The Pursuit of Knowledge

Listen to someone who pursued knowledge with a passion:

I devoted myself to search for understanding and to explore by wisdom everything being done under heaven. . . . I said to myself, "Look, I am wiser than any of the kings who ruled in Jerusalem before me. I have greater wisdom and knowledge than any of them." So I set out to learn everything from wisdom to madness and folly. But I learned firsthand that pursuing all this is like chasing the wind. The greater my wisdom, the greater my grief.

To increase knowledge only increases sorrow. (Ecclesiastes 1:13, 16-18)

In his bestselling book *Emotional Intelligence,* Daniel Goleman counters the popular idea that people's high IQ will place the world at their fingertips. Goleman's study led to the conclusion that "a high IQ is no guarantee of prosperity, prestige, or happiness in life." He goes on to cite a study of college graduates that showed no correlation between the graduates' IQ and their "salary, productivity, or status" or their "happiness with friendships, family, and romantic relationships." Goleman concludes that "at best, IQ contributes about 20 percent to the factors that determine life success, which leaves 80 percent to other forces."

Goleman's research confirms the Teacher's long-ago statement. Once again, the old cynic pierces our preconceptions to tell us that intelligence doesn't guarantee happiness and success is not guaranteed by knowledge and wisdom. We can be the smartest person in the world and still bumble through life. We can know everything there is to know and still be a failure.

Knowledge in the Garden

But the Teacher was not the first to burst the balloon. We should have learned the lesson from the Garden of Eden.

Humanity's fall from an intimate relationship with God took place when the humans ate the forbidden fruit of a tree. We all know that, but we often forget what kind of tree it was. Adam and Eve rebelled against God by eating from the tree of the knowledge of good and evil.

When the serpent tempted Eve, he cast his spell over her by telling her that the fruit of that tree would give her further knowledge: "You will be like God, knowing both good and evil" (Genesis 3:5). And when Adam and Eve ate, their knowledge did increase. In the words of the biblical text, "their eyes were opened" (v. 7) so that they knew they were naked. That's when they fled from each other and hid from God.

We can hear the Teacher say again, "The greater my wisdom, the greater my grief. To increase knowledge only increases sorrow."

Think of the tremendous strides humankind has made in just the past hundred years! We have gone from riding horses to driving cars to launching space shuttles. We have progressed from pencils to computers, from Pony Express to e-mail and faxes.

But have these unquestionably marvelous advances brought happiness and success to the world? Has the world grown in harmony and community? The answer is obvious. Pursuing intelligence under the sun is essentially meaningless.

If Not Intelligence, Then Wisdom

People who know the Bible well know that it puts a great premium on wisdom. The book of Proverbs says,

> Joyful is the person who finds wisdom
> the one who gains understanding. (3:13)

More to the point, the Bible seems to value wisdom specifically over intelligence or knowledge. What is the difference?

To be considered smart, a person usually has to know a lot of facts. Remember back to your school days as you prepared for tests. The teachers gave you large amounts of material that you had to memorize in order to succeed on the test. Early on, it might be a list of spelling words or multiplication facts. Later it was the battles of the Civil War. If you took a foreign language, then you had lists of vocabulary and grammatical rules to memorize.

As you progressed through the grades, learning became more than rote memorization. You needed to synthesize material, to understand principles and apply them to previously unseen problems. Nonetheless, even then, everything had its basis in knowing facts.

Biblical wisdom, on the other hand, is more like a skill. It is more a "knowing how" than a "knowing what." It is essentially the ability to have insight as to the best way to live life.

Indeed, in many ways biblical wisdom is similar to Goleman's concept of emotional intelligence. Emotional intelligence goes well beyond facts; it "includes self-control, zeal and persistence and the ability to motivate oneself."[2] It also features "abilities such as being able to motivate oneself and persist in the face of frustration; to control impulse and delay gratification; to regulate one's moods and keep distress from swamping the ability to think; to empathize and to hope."

Biblically wise people can navigate life successfully not only because they know many facts, but also because they know the right time to express their emotions and make decisions. They do not get buried in disappointment when they experience a setback. Rather, they look at the situation and have hope that things will get better. At the heart of wisdom is the ability to know the right time for a thought, an action or an emotion.

The Limits of Wisdom

The lure of wisdom is that it can bring us a successful life. It can provide a way for us to survive and thrive in an uncertain world. The Teacher at one point says as much, stating that both wisdom and money "are a benefit as you go through life. Wisdom or money can get you almost anything, but only wisdom can save your life" (7:11-12).

But elsewhere he acknowledges that you can't always depend on wisdom. Sometimes it lets you down:

> I have seen everything in this meaningless life, including the death of
> good young people and the long life of wicked people. So don't be too

good or too wise! Why destroy yourself? On the other hand, don't be too wicked either. Don't be a fool! Why die before your time? Pay attention to these instructions, for anyone who fears God will avoid both extremes. (7:15-18).

This passage is staggering when we pause to consider it. Did you ever imagine that the Bible would caution you to beware of being too good or too wise? But we must remember that the Teacher restricted his observations to truth as it is under the sun, apart from spiritual realities. And in that light, his observation strikes us as quite true. We know not only godly and wise people who suffer deeply, but also godless and foolish people who live blindly blissful lives.

Two people I know, Charles and Mark, illustrate this point quite well. Charles sacrificed dearly for the Lord. He had gifts and energy to create a wonderfully meaningful and prosperous life for himself in the United States, but he and his wife felt called into ministry overseas. They ministered for years in Asia, and as a result of their self-denying labors, many people came to the Lord. Today Charles is still relatively young and continues to sacrificially serve the Lord.

Charles, a wise servant of God, sacrificed dearly for his Lord. And how has the Lord rewarded this wise and good servant? Charles suffers from a host of diseases that may eventually take his life. His wife's health also suffers.

Mark, on the other hand, lives and prospers, although he has abused his body for years through various addictions. Mark's drunken driving has put him in jail a number of times and has even put a few people in the hospital. And yet he seems happy enough.

The End of Wisdom

Wisdom is no guarantee of the good life, the Teacher reminds us. But even if all godly wise people lived wonderful lives, he would say that striving to be wise is not worth it. He explains, "Yet I saw that the wise and the foolish people share the same fate. Both will die. So I said to myself, 'Since I will end up the same as the fool, what's the value of all my wisdom? This is all so meaningless!' For the wise and the foolish both die. The wise will not be remembered any longer than the fool" (2:14-16).

The great limitation of human wisdom is that death brings it to an end. Death is the great equalizer that puts all people on the same plane. Often God uses death or its near presence to awaken people to the small, insignificant part they play in the universe. It is this sober wisdom that Rosie offered Noah in plucking him from death.

Someone might respond, though, that wisdom and kindness will live on in memory and bless the following generations. The Teacher told a story to crush that hope:

> There was a small town with only a few people, and a great king came with his army and besieged it. A poor, wise man knew how to save the town, and so it was rescued. But afterward no one thought to thank him. So even though wisdom is better than strength, those who are wise will be despised if they are poor. What they say will not be appreciated for long. (9:14-16)

Smart and Foolish

Wisdom depends on our ability to know the right time and place for a word or an action. And yet there is clearly a limit to human wisdom. As the Teacher perceptively observed, "God has made everything beautiful for its own time. He has planted eternity in the human heart, but even so, people cannot see the whole scope of God's work from beginning to end" (Ecclesiastes 3:11).

The Teacher was not a fool. Indeed, he was recognized by many as a wise man (Ecclesiastes 12:9). And though he recognized the limits of human wisdom, he also recognized the advantages of wisdom over foolishness: "So I decided to compare wisdom with foolishness and madness. . . . I thought, 'Wisdom is better than foolishness, just as light is better than darkness. For the wise can see where they are going, but fools walk in the dark'" (2:12-14).

With this vivid metaphor of sight and blindness, the Teacher did acknowledge that in some sense wisdom can be a guide to life. He describes the fool is someone who tries to live life with a blindfold, knocking into the furniture and sore shins. The wise can walk confidently and safely through life because their eyes are wide open, seeing all the obstacles before they run into them.

And intelligence, remember, is not the same thing as wisdom. Some of the most intelligent and learned people in the world can be the blindest of fools—especially if their intelligence is combined with pride and defensiveness. Noah, though brilliant in his own field, was incredibly foolish in other aspects of his life. People with even a dime's worth of sense know when something is wrong with their inner world and their relationships. And Noah didn't have a clue about that. Though brilliant, he was both blind and foolish . . . until God used a traumatic mugging and the influence of an old Jewish couple to open his eyes. And this, for Noah, was the beginning of true wisdom.

Restoring Wisdom Through Relationship

Noah came to face one simple truth: Knowledge and accomplishment that takes us to greater self-sufficiency is, in fact, rubbish. It leads to self-righteousness and in turn to blindness. Most of us must be rescued from blind foolishness, as Noah was, before we begin to see the light.

The Bible contains a particularly eloquent story of how this works. It's the story of Job, who faced a period of testing that cost him his wealth, his family and his health. Job and his friends tried to grapple with this predicament through the power of their human wisdom, their understanding of how life worked.

To these friends, the wise conclusion was obvious: Job's suffering was the result of his sin. The solution was equally obvious to them: Job needed to repent. The problem was that Job knew that his losses were not due to disobedience. And though he did not know the reason why he suffered, Job did have his own idea of the wise course of action: he would confront God with the injustice God had perpetrated against him.

In one sense, Job got what he wanted, a meeting with God. But Job was ill prepared for what that signified. Job had wanted to place God on trial, to challenge what Job perceived God had done to him. Instead, God put Job on trial, asking:

> Who is this that questions my wisdom
>   with such ignorant words?
> Brace yourself like a man,
>   because I have some questions for you,
>   and you must answer them. (Job 38:2-3).

In the next four chapters of the book of Job, God goes on to question Job's wisdom and presents his own. He asks Job a series of questions about the making and running of the universe. God also describes the way he endows some creatures with wisdom while withholding it from others (e.g., the ostrich in Job 39:13-18).

What is God really telling Job? What is he asking Job to do? The answer is implied in Job's response to God:

> I know that you can do anything,
>   and no one can stop you.
> You asked, "Who is this that questions my wisdom with such
>   ignorance?"
>   It is I—and I was talking about things I knew nothing about,
>   things far too wonderful for me. . . .
> I take back everything I said,
>   and I sit in dust and ashes to show my repentance." (Job 42:2-6)

And so Job's response to God's challenge is to surrender to Wisdom himself. He has learned the lesson God intends for all of us—that wisdom does not lie in knowledge or even understanding. Wisdom is a *relationship*. In the words of C. S. Lewis: "I know now, Lord, why you utter no answer. You are yourself the answer. Before your face questions die away."

Consider the motto that begins the book of Proverbs: "Fear of the LORD is the foundation of true knowledge" (Proverbs 1:7). We often misunderstand the book of Proverbs as a book about learning or knowing certain things. But it, too, is really a book about a relationship. The book is structured in a way that forces us to remember that the pithy principles presented in chapters 10 through 31 should never be read out of the context of the first nine chapters and their key message that all true wisdom is rooted in a relationship with God.

If we read Proverbs from the perspective of the New Testament, moreover, we know that wisdom is found in Christ. The apostle Paul understood this. Speaking of Jesus, he said, "In him lie hidden all the treasures of wisdom and knowledge" (Colossians 2:3).

The bottom line of human knowledge is simple: we can't know it all. Indeed, we can know only a very little about God's vast and rich creation. Awareness of our limitations should breed humility and dependence. For true wisdom is found only where Job found it: in surrender to God.

Shrewd as Snakes

All of this is not to say that intellect, intelligence, knowledge and human wisdom are bad. Far from it. Our minds are truly divine gifts, to be fully used in the service of God and one another. The trouble, in this fallen world, is that people so often use these gifts to their own prideful and selfish ends. Many, even Noah was at times, are as ready to harm others as to help them.

How should we react to this reality? Jesus had these words of wisdom for his disciples as he sent them out into the world: "I am sending you out like sheep among wolves. Therefore be as shrewd as snakes and as innocent as doves" (Matthew 10:16 NIV).

First, we should not become like prideful and self-centered hoarders of knowledge. As we go out among the wolves, we need to remain sheep. We need to remain aware of the limits of our wisdom and to retain our innocence, our humility and our dependence on God and one another.

But in another sense we need to be as shrewd as snakes. To be shrewd is to keep a wary eye on the other person. To be shrewd is to recognize the other person may try to harm us and be prepared to defend ourselves. (The snake metaphor also suggests that we should try not to be predictable in our interactions but should rather get people to consider the truth in unexpected ways.)

Christians need to hear this message as it relates to our wisdom and intelligence. To be humble and dependent does not mean to sacrifice our intelligence to our faith. If we do, we betray our faith, which claims not only our hearts but also our minds.

Evangelical Christianity has a reputation as being anti-intellectual, and sometimes this charge is true. But the Bible suggests things should be otherwise.

Two passages have always motivated me in this regard. The apostle Peter encourages us to "always be prepared to give an answer to everyone who asks you to give the reason for the hope that you have" (1 Peter 3:15 NIV). And Paul, describing the life of the mind as a battle, commands us to "take captive every thought to make it obedient to Christ" (2 Corinthians 10:5 NIV).

Christians are blessed with the mind of Christ as well as gifted with minds of our own. We have a responsibility to use every resource we have—our own minds included—to reflect his wisdom to the rest of the world.

Wisdom Above the Sun

We cannot find a more powerful and eloquent exposition of the difference between wisdom under the sun and wisdom above the sun than that which Paul gives us in 1 Corinthians 1:18—2:16. The wisdom of the cross, Paul says, is "foolishness" to the wisdom of the world. In the same measure, God has made the wisdom of the world's philosophers, scholars and debaters foolish and has "shown their wisdom to be useless nonsense."

Fear of God, the open-mouthed awe that puts him first in our lives, compels us to recognize that all true wisdom comes from God. Getting along in life does not depend on our native intelligence or our knowledgeable degrees or even our human wisdom. It depends on our willingness to embrace God's wisdom, even though that willingness may lead us to appear foolish to others.

God has chosen not to provide a system of thought that proves his existence. In the Bible he has revealed himself not primarily through logic but through story, paradox, insight and metaphor. And in the world he comes to us through the witness of creation, the redemptive sacrifice of his Son, and the ongoing ministry of the Holy Spirit.

All this means that knowing God does not depend on our IQ. In fact, a genius may not recognize God, while a young child knows God intimately. A brilliant physicist may discover things about the constitution of matter that no other mortal can see or even understand, but a mentally impaired person can still know the God who created all matter.

Above the sun, we find wisdom in the Word—and the Word is first of all a person, Jesus Christ. Wisdom above the sun, in other words, is a relationship. And that person who is Wisdom has spoken to us wise words. Fear of God drives us to those words, which we find in the Bible. The whole Bible then becomes a divinely inspired guide as we navigate life. It not only gives us guidelines and principles, but also engenders in us a mindset or worldview that lifts us above our own limited perspective to enable us to see ourselves, others and our world from the viewpoint of God himself.

In this light, our fear of God energizes our attempts to learn about God's world in the light of his Word, to expand our knowledge and understanding in response to his wisdom. God's people, therefore, should be the world's most passionate learners as we explore the wonders of his creation, contemplate the complexities of life, and marvel at the majesty of our Creator.

Taking a Closer Look

Reread Ecclesiastes 1:18.
Give examples from your life when increased wisdom has led to increased grief.

Reread Ecclesiastes 2:12-16.
What concrete advantages does wisdom have over folly? Why does the

Teacher judge wisdom as ultimately meaningless? In your opinion, is he right?

How Do We Chase Wisdom?

1. Who is the wisest human being you know? What makes him or her so wise?

2. What can you do to gain wisdom?

3. What benefits are derived from education, from learning new skills?

4. What skills and abilities are of most value to you for practical day-to-day living?

5. In what ways does God give his children wisdom to live life successfully?

6. What does it mean to live a successful life?

7. What Scripture passages help ground you in God's wisdom?

6

CHASING AFTER SPIRITUALITY

"My Spiritual Life Will Save Me"

The alarm clock clattered, and Noah reached over and silenced it with his usual early-morning swat. He lay in bed and once again fought the urge to stay there forever. Then he remembered he was supposed to have breakfast with Jack—and realized with surprise he was looking forward to it.

He arrived at the diner twenty minutes early. He always liked to be the first one there, to claim his space and get set up before the other person arrived. He sat back in the red vinyl booth and smiled. He liked this place—a deliberate throwback to the fifties and the happy days of leisurely breakfasts, carefree orders not restricted by cholesterol, and women with hair that could hold a small hammer, let alone a number-two pencil.

He had already started on his second cup of coffee when Jack pushed through the glass door. "Jack, it's good to see you. Thanks for meeting me this early."

Jack nodded. "I see you've started without me."

"Just warming up the table. You want coffee?"

"Are you kidding? It's one addiction I see no reason to break, or even worry about. Couldn't start another day in this world without it."

Their banter continued until the waitress slapped down the plastic menus and waited for them to order. When she finished her scribbling and sailed off for the kitchen, Noah took a deep breath.

"Look, Jack, I don't know yet how to explain what happened to me in New York

or even how to explain what has happened since I got back. All I know is I want something more with God, in my marriage, and—I think—in life. And, well . . ."

Jack leaned forward, silently urging Noah on. Noah winced and tried again.

"Okay. Now, I think you know I have been a Christian who believed all the truths without really taking them seriously. Not a hypocrite exactly, but I certainly didn't give my spiritual life much priority. I guess you'd say—"

"Let me interrupt for a second," Jack said. "Do you want to talk about what happened in New York?" Jack asked. "Or about where you are with God right now? I guess I'm a bit confused about what you want to do here."

"Me too," Noah said softly. "Look, I know I am at the beginning of a major change. I have to head in a different direction with Joan, with God. I know that, but I just don't know what that means or what it looks like. If you asked me to give an analysis of a stock, I could tell you about its profit margin, what its competition is doing, and what issues it faces in this quarter. But put me in a position to reevaluate my life, and I'm just . . . lost. Where do I begin?"

Jack's well-starched shirt crinkled as he put his elbows on the table. "Noah, if you had asked me this question six months ago, I would have laid out a Bible study plan, told you about a prayer seminar that is coming to town in a few weeks, and helped you map out a time, place and procedure to develop spiritual discipline. And six months ago I would have left this breakfast and felt as if great things are going to happen because you are finally on track. What I mean is, I used to believe there was a clear, relatively simple path to growing spiritually. And I still think there are some crucial things you need to know and do in a disciplined way. That's how I have lived my Christian life, and I would have told you it was not only the right way, but the way to be right with—Noah, is something wrong?"

Noah jerked upright and realized his mind had wandered. He had always felt that Jack talked too much. "No, uh . . . sorry. Go on."

Jack looked away. He seemed momentarily distracted. He did not continue, and the silence hung thick between them. Normally Noah would have rushed in to fill the gap with a change of conversation, but this time he resisted.

Jack looked back at Noah and finally spoke. "I'm just not sure, Noah, that what I'm about to say is fair to you. You're just now rethinking the direction of your life, *and this might throw a roadblock in your way. The thing is, I've been going through a significant struggle too, and the truths I would have offered to you with utter confidence six months ago—the ones I want to talk about now—seem, well, a tad hollow. More noise than real substance."*

He paused and let another bubble of silence well up. "All right. Noah, let me put you on the spot. Do you want me to talk about what I have been through the last six months? I want to answer your question about what to do to find God's purposes for you, but I just can't do that the same way I would have done several months ago."

Noah took a gulp of cooling coffee to cover his discomfort. "Look, I didn't think a matter this big would be settled by the time both of us have to go to work. So, yes, absolutely. Tell me what has happened to you."

Jack sat back. "Crap."

"What?"

"That's it—crap has happened to me. Lots and lots of it, piling up on my well-groomed garden. I know plants need fertilizer, but when the pile is four feet tall and six feet wide and the wind is blowing the wrong way and your air conditioner . . . Well, you get my drift. What happened is actually simple to describe, but what it has done to me is hard to explain. I don't want to compare it to your accident, but I do see some similarities.

"Six months ago, the man who was my spiritual mentor, a pastor who befriended me when I joined my first law practice, left his wife. He's having an affair with a woman who was on the staff of his church. He called me recently to ask if I knew anyone who might offer him a job. I listened to him, and I could not believe my ears. I mean, this man has a doctorate in theology from one of the most conservative seminaries in the country. He has taught in Christian schools, served on the board of a major mission, been a pastor for twenty-five years. What can I say? I've patterned my life after that man ever since I was in my midtwenties. Honestly, I could kill—oh, there we are."

The waitress had arrived with their order. Jack looked at his plate, picked up his fork, then put it down again. "I can't tell you how many times I've been warned, 'Don't let your faith rest on any human, only on the finished work of Christ.' But if our faith doesn't depend on each other to some degree, then I don't really know why it matters for us to meet together."

Noah stopped Jack. "But he simply wasn't being consistent with what he taught you, right? If he had been, he wouldn't have fallen away from the Lord."

Jack sighed. "Yeah. Maybe. I don't think it's that simple, though. Do the right thing and right things happen. Do the wrong thing and bad things will come your way. I don't know if I believe that anymore. Look, I'm not giving up on spiritual truths or discipline. It just seems like our human capacity for self-deception is far bigger than I ever realized. Anyway, I guess you and I are both more committed to rules and systems than we are to living in faith."

Noah's attention sharpened. "What are you talking about?"

"I mean we are both men who can't bear losing control. Frankly, any intimate relationship requires more humility, more openness, pain and trust than either of us is capable of giving. Right?"

Noah's eyes narrowed and his brow shot up. "Hey, speak for yourself." He relaxed into a wry grin. "But my irritation at what you're saying probably indicates you're right."

Jack laughed gently. "Noah, do you even know how often you get irritated with me? If I had a ten-dollar bill for each time I have seen that look, I could retire and send your kids through college."

Noah flushed and changed the subject. "So what do you think happened with your friend?"

Jack exhaled quickly. "Don't know. But what I've noticed after being a Christian for thirty years is that Christians are not all that different from our so-called secular counterparts. Oh, we believe we are going to heaven. But we have just as many if not more egotists, arrogant know-it-alls, and thin-skinned hotheads among us than the average law firm. And most of us don't have the slightest idea how to deal with our teenage daughters or our money or our lonely wives.

Jack looked Noah squarely in the face. "And me—I have a spiritual façade as phony as a cheap motel. I think you can just call it self-righteousness."

Noah flinched. The waitress towered above them with a pot of coffee in each hand. If she had not overheard the conversation, she had at least caught the intense *mood. She seemed unusually quiet and even respectful.*

"You guys want any more java?"

"No," Jack replied softly, "I'll take the check."

"You got it," She snapped her gum thoughtfully as she reached for her order pad, then realized she needed something from the register. "Be right back."

"Jack, I'm not a dumb man," Noah said as she squeaked away in her rubber-soled shoes. "Usually I'm fairly quick at getting the gist of a conversation. But I'm still missing what you're trying to say to me here."

Jack scratched his starchy shirtsleeve. "Someday I'm going to wear a jean shirt to work and see if anyone has a heart attack." He paused and pushed the ruffled edges of his fried eggs into the untouched portion of his hash browns. He seemed distracted, and Noah didn't know whether to be quiet or to ask his question again. Jack looked up. "Noah, we both know that Joan has been very lonely and afraid to ask for much or tell you how unhappy she's been. True?"

Noah was not surprised by the question, but he had no idea where Jack was going with it. "Well, yes. I don't know how afraid Joan is or has been, but I can tell you I think she is having more trouble with me this last week than she has had in a long time. So what's your point?"

"Simple. You and I usually dictate the agenda. We are men who are used to getting our way. And I'm no better at relating to my wife than you are at relating to Joan. If you asked Marcia what it's like to be married to me, I think if she were honest, I think she'd say, 'He loves me . . . up to a point.' And when that point is reached, I draw the line and either evade the issue or somehow make her feel it's her problem.

"I wonder if that's what my mentor did. I suspect he just lived a little longer with some well-guarded lies than he could bear. Maybe he had some sexual issues, but who doesn't? I think what really happened is that, over time, he used his religious systems to insulate himself from the truth about his own heart.

"What makes me sick is I never asked him the hard questions. I was as much a coward with him as I am at times with Marcia. I guess what I'm saying is I don't want that for you or for me.

Noah looked at Jack, and he felt warmth for a man who had been his senior, a distant guide he never took seriously enough to ask for help. He smiled. He had thought he'd come away from this meeting with a direction to pursue. Instead he thought he might have begun a friendship.

He wondered if the same might be true of his relationship with God.

𝕯

The conversation with Jack at breakfast played in Noah's mind for the whole ride to work. He didn't even notice he had not turned on the radio until he drove into the parking lot. The young executive who had parked in his spot a few weeks ago had taken the space next to his and parked over the line, so getting in and out of the space would be impossible.

Noah's hands clenched the steering wheel in irritation, then felt his annoyance drain away. He had other more important things to worry about.

His new position at the company put him in a strange position in his Chicago office. As head of analysis for the company as a whole, he set the philosophy for what would be bought and sold through the whole firm, and daily he had the ear of both Andrajian brothers. He did not run the day-to-day operations of the Chicago group, but if he made a two-minute phone call to one of the Brothers, a head would roll. He had the power to do whatever he wanted with the careers of people who a month ago had subtly ridiculed him in their weekly analysis meetings.

People like Jonathan Satterwhite.

Noah had endured the man's barely concealed disdain and patronizing remarks for years. And he had to admit he enjoyed Satterwhite's discomfort. He obviously expected to be fired at any minute, and he went to great lengths to avoid catching Noah's eye. When they were in the same room, he seemed to fade into his papers, staring at his well-ordered sheaf of reports as if looking for a holy grail.

And yes, Noah had fantasized about taking Jonathan apart limb by nasty limb. He couldn't help wanting to watch Jonathan suffer as he took away his corner office and then set him to tasks that men twenty years his junior would have found humiliating.

But Noah's conversations with Joan over the past few weeks had changed his heart. For the first time he shared with her about the hostile atmosphere at his office. Joan had never understood why some days Noah's shirts came back with the odor of the jungle on them. Those were the days he suffered the polished slurs of Jonathan and his colleagues with quiet, distant rage. Noah was the kind of angry man who sweated when he wanted to scream.

"Do you want to make them pay?" Joan had asked him just the other night. He had looked into her eyes, thought of the years of hurt he had subjected her to, and realized she hurt more for him than she did for herself. That killed the pleasure of his vengeance fantasies. All he really cared about now was getting the office on an even, productive keel.

Noah knew the office grapevine was filled with gossip of what he had done to gain his new position and what he was going to do to solidify his power. And frankly, he was getting tired of the gossip, invective and power grabbing. The limited pool of perks, including who parked in which spot and who got the most prestigious office, seemed more important to coworkers than how the company progressed. Each day when Noah entered the building and greeted the receptionist and the other office workers, he could see fear in their faces, uncertainty about whether or not they would have jobs the next week.

He saw the same look on the faces of his other associates, including Lee, his former boss. But they were gradually coming to terms with their new working relationships. The only one who still avoided his eyes was Jonathan Satterwhite. And Noah had decided it was time for the two of them to make peace as well.

As luck—or God—would have it, Jonathan turned the corner just as Noah walked in the door. Both men approached the same elevator. To turn away at this point would be too obvious, so both got on together.

They stood uncomfortably for long seconds, looking straight ahead. "Ah, good morning, Noah," Jonathan ventured as the doors closed.

Noah nodded. "Good morning, Jonathan. I'm glad I bumped into you. I've been summoned to New York to meet with the staff and the brothers, and I wanted to get an opinion on the MacKenzie deal before I left. Could you meet with me this morning?"

Jonathan knew he could no more say no to Noah than go to work shining shoes. He replied with jovial irritation: "No problem, Noah. You name the time."

For a split second, Noah considered responding in kind to the veiled sarcasm. Then he took a deep breath. "Look, Jonathan, you are a valuable and deeply respected associate. I know we've been at odds for years, but your analyses are weighty and, more often than not, correct. I don't want to put you in a position of rearranging your schedule for me. I simply want to know if you have time this morning to give me an update I can take to New York."

Jonathan's cheeks flamed. He had chosen a deferential tactic that allowed him to be the patronizing servant, but Noah's sincere praise had trumped his snide efforts. Jonathan coughed and looked away. "Sure, Noah, I understand. I just meant I'd be glad to meet with you at your convenience."

Noah smiled. "I'm going to be scribbling and reading this morning; you can drop in whenever you have a moment. If you don't, just let me know when you are available."

The elevator door opened, and Noah, who was closest to the door, stepped out quickly and strode toward his interior office. Out of the corner of his eye, he saw Jonathan hesitate, watching him, then lurch forward awkwardly as the doors close.

Noah stepped into his office and shook his head. He didn't know whether to laugh or cry. Jonathan obviously hated and feared him. He wanted to tell Jonathan all was forgiven and explain what God had done in his life over the last several weeks, but he suspected a frontal approach would put his colleague over the edge. There had to be a way to offer Jonathan the same kind of gift that his experience in New York had given him . . . but in small daily doses. And minus the mugging, of course.

Noah smiled at that thought and realized that the careful effort he put into reading a stock was the same energy he could offer to God in understanding Jonathan. It was going to be a very good day.

ᴆ

The Idol: "My Spiritual Life Will Save Me"

Many people today are turning their attention to spiritual matters. Books with words like *angels* or *God* in their titles have become bestsellers. More people than ever, it seems, are willing to admit that there is more to life than what we can see and touch. Many churches have record attendance.

It is not unusual for people to turn to religion in order to find meaning in their lives, especially when tragedy strikes or as they grow older. As men and women approach middle age, they have lived long enough to be disappointed. Relationships have let them down. Work may be tiring and unfulfilling, life confusing and overwhelming. Religion seems like a logical refuge from the mess of everyday living, a way to infuse significance into the circumstances of life.

Religion can certainly be a valid source of meaning. But it can also become an idol that leads people away from and not toward God.

Noah's experience in New York stirred something new in him, an awakening. The couple he followed for a few blocks reminded him that he was a lonely man, unskilled at intimacy. His brush with danger brought home the reality that he was mortal and left him wondering what his life meant. And his very success, the accomplishment of the dream he had worked so hard for, contributed to his new hunger for meaning. For it is not only age and tragedy that awakens us to "the more." Often it is a dream fulfilled. Once we achieve the long-awaited goal that has organized our life and provided the energy for our daily labor, we may well find ourselves face-to-face with an emptiness our striving had masked.

In a sense, Noah was set up by God. He was elated by his hard-earned success, touched by his encounter with Jakob and Rosie, and terrified by the experience of being mugged.

Few people experience such intense interactions. And yet no one escapes the call to consider the ultimate meaning of life in the light of tragedy and success. God sends all of us daily invitations to seek him out, to know him and trust him.

The trouble is, for many people, religion becomes a way for people to cope with life without actually knowing God.

The Pitfall of Smugness

My own story runs along these lines. For as far back as I remember, life worried me. I have no idea why I felt as I did. I had loving parents and lived in a safe community, but I grew up with a sense that other people—and certainly God—found me inadequate. From the time I was in elementary school, I struggled with intense guilt feelings and a fear of dying.

I sought refuge in the church. What could make better sense? I knew that "good" people went to church and followed its rules, and so that's where I went to find meaning. I met other good kids there and found myself feeling quite comfortable with the direction of my life, at least on the surface. But the empty feeling in the pit of my stomach would not go away.

Looking back, I now understand that I was not actually a Christian during this time, even though I was a model church member, especially for a teenager! I did everything right. I wasn't sneaking off with my friends for a beer or causing trouble at home for my parents. I was very moral, very religious—and very smug.

Smugness is the result of a religion of externals. It is a complacency that can develop only when we understand our connection with God to be the result of a to-do list.

Actually my list, like that of many other people, included more don'ts than dos.

Sure, I needed to do my chores, go to church, be nice to people, pray occasionally and perhaps read the Bible. But there were many other items I had to be careful *not* to do. I knew I wasn't supposed to swear, drink, lie, masturbate, or engage in any kind of sexual activity whatsoever. Nasty thoughts were harder to control, but I rationalized that nasty thoughts weren't as bad as nasty deeds.

Now I wasn't completely smug, because I was not perfect in my obedience. But I could get close. And don't most of those of us who operate with this concept of religion operate with a "goodness scale" idea of our worth? It's not that we are always good and right, but that we do more good things than bad things. Our good actions far outweigh our bad actions, and we think a reasonable God will have to take that into account. At least that's what I thought.

My Way or the Highway

Then gradually, over time, I fell into another kind of smugness. I started to believe I had a corner on how to approach God.

And I was not wrong to think that what I believed was right and biblical. But I was wrong to think there was only one right way to grow in faith. That assumption inevitably leads to the conclusion that if my way is right and true, then all other means of growth are wrong. That not only implies I cannot learn from other approaches. I must also resist them wholeheartedly . . . and force everyone else to fit into my mold.

My first clear lesson about this reality came in the context of a college fellowship. Dan and I went to college in the early seventies, at the beginning of the "Jesus Movement." Those were exciting times. We regularly saw our friends come to faith in Christ. During the first weeks of our freshman year at Ohio Wesleyan University, five of us started a weekly fellowship, and by the end of the school year, the group had grown to about a hundred students. Most of the new people were recently converted, including my old friend and roommate, Dan.

We began the second year with great enthusiasm. We had no adult leadership, but many of us had been Christians for awhile now. With our new maturity, we fully expected God to do great things.

Soon, however, we found that our maturing had taken us in different directions. Some of us had come under the influence of a Reformed theologian; to us worship had to be orderly and intellectual. Others had discovered the Holy Spirit and charismatic gifts; they felt that worship should be exciting and emotional. Others came under the influence of a Bible teacher who understood God's history of salvation as divided into discrete dispensations; to them speaking in tongues was of the devil.

The bickering began. How would worship be conducted? How would we encourage others to seek a relationship with God? Bickering turned into fighting, and soon separate groups were formed. Amazingly, God often worked around our pitiful theological infighting, and many people still came to know him. But the fact that we simply couldn't come together in Christian love and understanding set a disastrous example.

I am not saying that any approach to God is equally valid or that these three views of the Bible and faith are unequivocally or even equally legitimate. What is at issue here is the complete disdain we felt for each other and the incredible confidence we each had that our own approach to God was the right one.

Each of us was chasing after God through our own religious constructs, and at times the experience devolved to little more than being a fan of a particular sports team. We wanted our team to win and crush all the opponents. We had it right, everyone else had it wrong, and we found security and peace in this smug belief. In a word, we had God in a box of our own making.

It would take a while for God to shake me out of a "my way or the highway" attitude.

The Legalism Trap

What I and my friends had fallen into in college was actually a form of legalism. Legalism involves seeking spiritual fulfillment through our behavior only, performing religious acts based on fear or the belief that our lives will work out because we're doing what God wants.

In our story, Jack was just beginning to realize he had been living for a long time as a reasonable but true-blue legalist. His particular form of legalism was based on the belief that spiritual disciplines such as daily quiet time, a regular prayer list and tithing are not only necessary, but sufficient, for spiritual growth and regeneration. He had always held that if people carried out these practices faithfully, all would be well with them spiritually.

People from other traditions might believe that real maturity is reached only after we are delivered from satanic presence or can speak in tongues or get out of denial or propagate the theories of Christian leader X. Whatever the details, the underlying assumptions are the same: (1) Religious maturity involves a distinct event, level of knowledge, or act(s). (2) Once the person has experienced the event, reached the level of knowledge or done the act, he or she has reached religious maturity. (3) And once a person reaches religious maturity, he or she no will longer struggle with the internal conflict of the spirit and flesh.

So many times during my Christian life, I have been told that if only I would do this thing or that thing, I would experience fresh intimacy with God and mature as a Christian. Jack had been brilliant at offering such prescriptions to people. He was good with systems, setting up a plan of prayer, study and service. And people responded to these plans; they had liked knowing exactly what to do. But seldom had Jack asked hard questions about their relationships or their lives. He had seldom made any connection between their past, their current struggles and their relationship to God. Jack's systems had given people a false sense of control in the present rather than opening to them a vision of their past and future.

There is something undeniably attractive about a system that enables us to do right and avoid wrong. The problem lies in promoting one narrow view of spirituality, especially one focused on the externals rather than on the heart, and at the expense of other legitimate forms of spiritual expression. Such restrictions lead to smugness and self-righteous, a sense that we have God under our control. They can also lead to despair when we fail to measure up to what we believe is expected of us or when the legalistic system we follow proves inadequate for the tough issues of our lives.

And it will, because religious legalism is essentially a lie. Legalism is, at heart, idolatry.

From Passion to Idolatry

True spirituality is a relationship, not a system or a set of rules. And a relationship involves engaging our hearts in mystery, in the essential presence of another. That's especially true when it comes to knowing God. It's not a simple matter of doing right and avoiding wrong, but a dynamic process of engaging all that we are with the totality of who God has revealed himself to be in the Bible and in the world. It means loving him and worshiping him, struggling with him and surrendering to him.

God invites us to a passionate relationship where we experience our most profound confusion and rest, disappointment and joy. But all too often, as we see in the Old Testament story of the Israelites, we prefer to do things our own way.

God chose the Israelites to be his special people. They did nothing to deserve their status as God's people (Deuteronomy 7:7-11). God wanted their hearts, so he revealed his own heart to them. He made them wonderful promises, promises that he would never break.

God did put certain demands on his people. He asked them to offer sacrifices, to keep their vows, to pray, to be circumcised. God assured them of his loving presence in their midst by having his house, the temple, constructed in the most prominent place in their major city, Jerusalem. The Israelites could look to that building and say confidently, "God is here; we have nothing to fear. He will never allow anything to happen to us because of the temple."

Some Israelites abandoned their God (Yahweh) to worship idols, but most continued to participate in the worship of Yahweh—or at least to go through the motions. They were circumcised, and they had their children circumcised. They went to the temple and participated in the festivals. They even offered expensive sacrifices. They did everything a good Yahweh worshiper should do.

But gradually, perhaps subtly at first, their zeal for Yahweh was perverted into a zeal for religious appearances. The sacrifices they offered were intended not to express remorse over sin and love to Yahweh, but to put on a show of piety and perhaps wealth for neighbors ("I offered a bull; you can afford only a bird"). The temple itself, which Solomon said could not contain God, became a prison for him in the minds of the people. They believed they were invincible as long as they were connected to the temple because God wouldn't let his own glory be diminished.

The history of the Israelite people in the Old Testament reveals the same twisted desire that lurks in the hearts of almost all religious people. It is a desire to control God so we can manipulate him to serve us. And again, that is the heart of idolatry. Sinful, selfish people do not like the idea of a God who is more powerful than they are. Through idolatry we try to pare God down to our size.

The Folly of Religion

As we have seen, the Teacher desperately looked for meaning to life on earth. His desperation, however, did not allow him easy answers, and as a result, he did not find satisfaction in superficialities.

The Teacher looked to religion in the hope that meaning could be found there, but once again he was disappointed. He quickly recognized the idolatry of "religious" people. Let's listen to his observations and advice, because they expose the folly of so much religion.

> As you enter the house of God, keep your ears open and your mouth shut. It is evil to make mindless offerings to God. Don't make rash promises, and don't be hasty in bringing matters before God. After all, God is in heaven, and you are here on earth. So let your words be few. Too much activity gives you restless dreams; too many words make you a fool. When you make a promise to God, don't delay in following through, for God takes no pleasure in fools. Keep all the promises you make to him. It is better to say nothing than to make a promise and not keep it. Don't let your mouth make you sin. And don't defend yourself by telling the Temple messenger that the promise you made was a mistake. That would make God angry, and he might wipe out everything you have achieved. (5:1-6)

The Teacher blasted those smug Israelites who would make religion a matter of dos and don'ts. He condemned the public display that merely went through the motions of religion.

The religious people he observed offered the required sacrifices. They paid for the animals, took them up to the temple, and with great ostentation offered them to God. They took vows, promised impressive gifts, prayed long and fancy prayers. They received the blessing of the community for being good, Yahweh-worshiping people. After all, hadn't God asked for sacrifices, vows and prayers?

But the Teacher saw through these people's intentions and motives. Their sacrifices were not from the heart; they were "mindless." The prayers of the people were flowery, but they revealed no real passion for God.

The Teacher reminded such superficial religious people that "God is in heaven, and you are here on earth" (5:2). In other words, you don't have God under control by your superficial spirituality. You cannot manipulate God by your religious actions, and as a result your legalistic religion will not bring you satisfaction and peace.

Centuries later, when he was on earth, Jesus ran into people with a similar mindset. He had some very hard things to tell these people:

> What sorrow awaits you teachers of religious law and you Pharisees. Hypocrites! For you are so careful to clean the outside of the cup and the dish, but inside you are filthy—full of greed and self-indulgence! . . . What sorrow awaits you teachers of religious law and you Pharisees. Hypocrites! For you are like whitewashed tombs—beautiful on the outside but filled on the inside with dead people's bones and all sorts of impurity. (Matthew 23:25-27)

The Pharisees, according to the New Testament, were a highly religious group who scrupulously tended to all the minute details of their religion. They did everything that the law and their customs required of them. Jesus condemned them, not for falling short of their ideal, but for their smug self-righteousness . . . and for missing the whole point of true faith.

A Heart of Passion

Of course, the Teacher and Jesus both speak of a religion of externals; that is, a religion that requires only actions and not a heart of passion. This is legalistic religion, religion that seeks to control God and assumes he is utterly transparent and predictable. It says, "If I am good, then God will bless me. If I am not good, then something bad will happen to me."

We often labor to make the Christian life into a formula: obedience equals blessing and disobedience equals curse. But is this the way life really works? The Teacher points out what our experience teaches us daily: Good people often suffer, and bad people often prosper—"the death of good young people and the long life of wicked people" (7:15).

Superficial and legalistic religion is just as dangerous today as it was in the Teacher's time. We can find countless approaches to God and the spiritual life, each approach promising success and happiness if a series of steps are performed or principles are understood. The self-help industry has infringed on true spirituality by offering the secrets to a happy, satisfied, mostly problem-free faith. Everywhere about us is the implicit promise that God is in the business of securing our earthly well-being if we merely do the right things.

Take Jack, for instance. He became a Christian when he was in law school. His whole attitude toward life changed. He had his vitality back and entered into a steady process of learning to follow Christ through prayer, Bible study and consistent church work. Jack felt that life was finally under control. There was nothing that could bring him down. He knew God, and he knew what God expected from him.

But even before Jack learned about his mentor's affair, he began to feel an acute lack of excitement and joy. He didn't know it, but he was worn down by years of working with other Christians. He assumed he needed to work harder and to reemploy the techniques he had learned to keep his spiritual life fresh and alive. And renewed attention to "the basics" did work to increase his spiritual vigor. But the news of his mentor's affair cut deeply and sapped much of his enthusiasm.

When Jack started the Ecclesiastes Bible study, he was vaguely aware that his life—and his religion—was not working. What he didn't realize was that God was calling him away from legalism and into the relationship of true spirituality.

The Teacher disturbed him, but deep down he found solace, strange comfort in the radical message that life, including his spiritual life, was not as predictable as he had thought it was supposed to be. He regretted the years of offering others advice and direction based on the legalistic assumption that we can somehow control God.

Jack's meeting with Noah prompted him to see that walking in uncertainty and struggling with God's mystery might actually take both of them further than merely offering his old standard lines for following God. Jack is a case study in the movement from the first flames of spiritual passion to smugness and legalism to emptiness and back to a deeper, more vital kind of faith.

From Smugness to Emptiness

Smugness results from thinking we have God figured out. We know what he wants, we do it, and he blesses us. The "how-to" list may differ from person to person, but it could include going to church, reading the Bible, praying, fasting, regular repentance, attendance at small groups, memorizing a confession of faith and on and on. As difficult as some of these demands may be, they are still controllable requirements from a predictable God. Smugness is the reward for just going through the motions.

Smug people can't think too deeply about the true state of their hearts. That would lead to disaster. However, maintaining the pretense is hard to do in a fallen world. Illness inevitably strikes—or family conflict or financial difficulty. We break the rules and struggle with guilt or just a brooding sense that something is wrong. Life gives us periodic lessons that, no matter how hard we try, we cannot control life, even through our chosen mode of spirituality. And God is always working to unsettle our all-too-complacent view of ourselves and draw us into true relationship

Allow me to return to my own story. God had blessed me. I had good friends in the fellowship. I won a starting position my senior year on our state championship football team. I had an attractive girlfriend, Dianne, from the church.

In the spring, however, Dianne informed me she did not want a serious relationship with a man who wanted to be a minister because that was not a lifestyle she wanted. We broke up, and smugness turned to emptiness. I remember losing interest in church. Life just did not seem worth it any longer. I didn't know it then, but God was moving me out of my legalistic idolatry and toward an authentic relationship with him.

God will not allow himself to be boxed in. He does not want our superficial worship. He will not tolerate our complacency. He will take our smugness and turn it to emptiness. By doing this, he will show us that he does not want our proper actions. He wants our hearts.

The prophets and poets made this clear in terms of Old Testament worship. Psalm 51, for instance, is the prayer of a formerly smug David. After his initial, intimate relationship with God, David had grown complacent and was serving God just on the surface, as the sin with Bathsheba indicated. But God revealed David's hidden rebellion, and this psalm is a testimony to his rekindled passion:

> You do not desire a sacrifice,
>> or I would offer one.
> You do not want a burnt offering.
> The sacrifice you desire is a broken spirit.
>> You will not reject a broken and repentant heart, O God. (vv. 16-17)

I learned this lesson myself as I moved from my legalistic smugness to the emptiness of life having gone awry. Little did I realize that God was setting the stage for an earth-moving transformation in my life. After a few months of listlessness, I happened on a different view of what following God could mean. A friend explained that Christianity is not an institution or a lifestyle; but a relationship with a person, Jesus Christ. It was not a matter of doing things to please him, but of giving myself to him—loving him with all my heart, all my soul, all my strength and all my mind (Luke 10:27).

That was the point where I turned from my smugness, from my legalistic, idolatrous religion, That was when I turned my life over to Christ.

Focus on Jesus

My conversion was not the end of the story of my pursuit of God, but the beginning. While my relationship with Christ has grown over the years, I have also experienced troubling and lonely times when I struggled to find new answers to my spiritual dilemma . . . and times when I fall back into legalism. I'll realize something is wrong in my life and I'll start thinking it's because I don't pray enough. Before I know it, I'm back to the dos and the don'ts. Legalism, in one sense, feels burdensome, but its attraction is that it is controllable; it is something I can do.

But God keeps us unsettled. He will not allow us to get complacent. And when God does break through our smugness in this way, he prods us to remember it is not the *form* but rather the *encounter* that is important. It is not how much we pray, how well we know the Bible, but how these things lead us into a more intimate relationship with him.

God himself reveals and conceals himself to us in a variety of ways. By doing so, he leaves us with a sense of wonder tinged with mystery. When we lose that sense of mystery, our wonder turns cynical. When we lose our sense of wonder, the mystery can confuse us.

Our approach to God must be open for surprises. This does not mean we have no direction at all. God does tell us pretty clearly what we should do. A life with no prayer or Scripture reading or fellowship with believers is a paltry existence at best. But to say that you need to have a quiet time at the beginning of the day to get right with God or that you must speak in tongues to really experience the Holy Spirit are oppressive requirements imposed by legalistic standards, not by God himself.

On the other hand, God does forbid certain things in his worship. A notable instance of this is the prohibition to make and worship an image, even of the true God (Exodus 20:4-6). We must know the Scriptures well enough to know what God desires and what he doesn't. But within these basic parameters, God gives us tremendous freedom in our approach to God. So we need to be careful what requirements we place on ourselves and especially on others.

I recently had a phone call from a man named Travis. Travis landscapes a large retreat center. He has a passionate heart for God, but he contacted me because he was deeply concerned that he might have to give up a practice that had nourished him for years. Once a week, Travis would get up and go to a secluded part of the retreat center. He would pray and read Scripture, and then at the end of his time of intimacy with God, he would take a bit of wine and bread, remember the death of Christ for his sins and give thanks.

He did not consider this Communion, a sacrament that he took regularly at our church. He did not tell many people about his private time of worship, and he never insisted that other people do this to get close to God. But one of the church leaders heard about this practice and told him he had to stop it. He said only a pastor could oversee this practice.

For a month, Travis was emotionally torn, not able to draw close to the Lord. Finally, however, he realized that he was giving in to the expectations of other people, not the Bible. He joyfully resumed his quiet-time practice.

Spirituality Above the Sun

Above the sun, we get a sense of God's mystery and unpredictability. We know God, to be sure, but we do not know him exhaustively. His unpredictability does not mean that he is arbitrary, but that we can never reduce his goodness and majesty to a trite formula.

Our above-the-sun perspective means we cannot presume to manipulate God through our rituals. We will not only encounter him in the expected places; he will also surprise us where we would least expect him.

Under the sun, our predictable view of God will lead eventually to smugness, then emptiness. God wants better for us than superficial religion. He will smash the idol we have made for him and reveal himself to us in ever richer tones. Our worship will then moves from smugness to passion as we learn to look for him in every aspect of our existence.

Our present experience of spirituality is intended to be a mere prelude to heaven. We really know little about heaven, but one thing we know is that our worship continues. We will see the Lord face-to-face, but the surprise and wonder and mystery will never stop:

No longer will there be a curse upon anything. For the throne of God and of the Lamb will be there, and his servants will worship him. And they will see his face, and his name will be written on their foreheads. And there will be no night there—no need for lamps or sun—for the Lord God will shine on them. And they will reign forever and ever. (Revelation 22:3-5)

Taking a Closer Look

Reread Ecclesiastes 5:1-6.

1. What advice does the Teacher give here? Is it good advice?

2. If the Teacher were speaking at your church or Bible study, how would he word his concern about religion?

How Do We Chase After Spirituality?

1. When is religion harmful? Can Christianity be harmful?

2. One philosopher accused religion of being the "opiate of the people," and another said that religion is "spiritual alcohol." What did they mean, and do they have any basis at all for their statements?

3. What is the difference between a superficial religion and a religion of the heart?

4. How can you tell true religion from false religion?

5. What does it mean to "put God in a box"?

6. What is the difference between contentment and smugness in religion?

7. In what ways has your spiritual life become out of balance?

8. What Scripture passages give you direction as you seek a more meaningful relationship with Christ?

7

CHASING AFTER IMMORTALITY

"I Will Have a Long Life
If I Take Care of My Body"

As soon as Noah got to work, he checked his voice mail. The first five messages were routine and required little more than a brief note to get the information needed to answer the questions. The sixth message was from Jakob, Rosie's husband. It was a halting voice that seemed unfamiliar with the procedure of leaving a message on voice mail.

"Mr. Adamson, I'm Jakob Harkowitz. My wife is Rosie. You gave me your number, and I do not want to disturb you; but my Rosie is in the hospital, and she asked that I call you. If you will be in New York any time soon, she hoped you might give her a call. Her number is 212-930-4500, room 1415. Thank you. Again, I hope I have not disturbed you."

Noah immediately picked the phone up and called the number. Jakob answered.

"Jakob, this is Noah Adamson. The man your wife saved from the mugging a few weeks ago."

"Yes. I am so glad you called me back."

"How are you? How is Rosie?"

"Well, Noah, this is the reason I have called you. Rosie, she wants to see you. Her cancer has worsened. But she is a stubborn woman. How else do you think she could live with me all these years? But the pain got worse, much worse. I know you are a very important man and busy, but Rosie felt that she had to see you before—"

"Jakob, I'm so sorry." Noah's eyes filled with tears. "I will be there this evening."

It was not even eight o'clock in the morning, and Noah's head spun in circles. He had begun to feel solid and alive. His recent conversations with Joan had been the best of his marriage, and his talk with Jack that morning had opened up a new vista of friendship he had never even considered, let alone thought possible. The drive to work had been one of the most pleasant in years, with a breeze blowing through the car window, and his encounter with Jonathan Satterwhite had left him feeling pleased.

But now he wanted to go back to bed. The cool wind had been replaced by the nearly silent drone of the air being driven through the ventilation system. The airy hope that filled him after his talk with Jonathan had vanished. Noah sat back in his chair, put his hands behind his head, closed his eyes. Then he opened them again. He would have to move quickly if he wanted to get to New York that day.

⅚

The cab ride to the hospital was ordinary and terrifying. Noah braced himself at each reckless stop and held his ground with every swerve. He spent the early part of the ride talking to Joan on his cell. Noah had only recently realized that his wife was a woman of keen spiritual sensitivity. A week ago he would not have been interested in her prayer life if it had slapped him in the face.

But all that had changed.

"Honey, I hate to tell you this, but I'm in New York. I got a phone call at the office from Jakob, the husband of the woman who saved my life. I tried to call you before I left Chicago, but you weren't home. Here is the news. Rosie is in the hospital. Her cancer has worsened. I don't know what to expect, and I wanted you to pray for me."

"Noah, slow down. You're going to the hospital? Let's think about what you need to take. I think you should stop at a florist—"

The phone sputtered and crackled. Noah could hear Joan's voice come in and out, but he could not make out another word after she suggested going to a florist. It was an idea that would not have come to him if he had thought about it for hours. He said goodbye in case she could hear. Then he flipped the phone closed. It felt *good to hear her voice, even her worry for him. But now he felt it was time to be alone and turn his heart to this strange God who had rescued him.*

What should he say to Jakob and Rosie? How was he to speak to people he had thought about and imagined for weeks but had never really talked to longer than a few minutes?

The cab dropped him off in front of Riverside Hospital in the Bronx. The ride had been quicker than he expected, and he had a few extra minutes. He used the time to walk down the block to a florist. He chose a bouquet that matched the scarf and dress Rosie had worn the day of the mugging. He wanted to make her happy. He felt a deep resolve to do whatever he could do to bring her joy.

Carrying the flowers, he had the sudden, absurd notion that he was about to ask Rosie to marry him. He recalled proposing to Joan, and he felt a sudden wave of distress. He had asked her to marry him with the passion of an engineer asking for the specs of a building site, and he had plucked away any excitement from the moment by adding that he didn't know if he wanted children and if that was a problem, the relationship could end with no hard feelings.

He felt sick at how little color and fragrance he had brought into Joan's life, even now. Somehow Rosie and her adoring husband had brought more romance and passion to his marriage and more conviction to his soul than all the sermons he had heard, or avoided listening to.

He crossed the hospital lobby, consulted the directory, and located the elevator that would take him to her room. The door opened at the fourteenth floor, and before Noah could walk off the elevator, he was pushed against the back wall by the odor. It was unlike any smell he had encountered. It was thick and coated with an antiseptic cleanness, but he knew it was the smell of death.

He wanted to push the button to descend back into the bright, busy world. He stood in the elevator until the doors began to close. Then he hit the button to open them again. He did this several times until a couple showed up in front of the elevator, clearly intending to get on. Noah gave them a nod and stepped out.

Room 1415 was at the far end of the hall. Instead of stalling when he got to the door, Noah sniffed the flowers once and walked in. It was a semiprivate room, but only one bed was occupied. Rosie was asleep, her breathing labored. Noah, who had only seen her once, barely recognized her pale, drawn face.

Jakob sat by the window in a metal chair with a green plastic cushion. He turned his head when Noah walked into the room and stood; he had clearly had been looking for Noah to arrive. He put his finger quickly to his lips, took Noah by the arm and led him back into the hallway.

"How is she?" Noah whispered.

"Not good. Not good."

Noah wanted to run but Jakob had not loosened his grip. He held Noah like an anchor in the midst of a gale. Noah looked into Jakob's weary face and asked: "How long, Jakob?"

Jakob dropped his eyes. "I'm told soon. But soon is not an answer, is it? I don't suppose anyone knows, do we, when life will pass. But soon means moments must linger longer that we normally allow. She wanted to see you to say thank you for giving her life one last moment of hope."

Noah's eyes filled with tears at the thought. He had come to thank her for being the hand of God; she wanted to bless him for allowing her to give one last time.

Noah spoke quietly. "Jakob, I have much to say to you and Rosie. You know she saved my life. But I want you to know you both saved me—my marriage, my soul. I know this makes no sense, not even to me, but I can't thank you enough. I don't know how to show my gratitude, but what I do have to offer in this strange city is some power that I can put at your disposal to give her the best, and I mean the finest, medical care the city has to offer. One phone call, and I can have the best oncologist here in a day. Jakob, will you let me do whatever I can for you both?"

Jakob smiled. His sadness and weariness didn't quench the warmth in his eyes. "Noah, she will be gone within a matter of weeks, at best. I know it would matter to you—I see it in your eyes—to help her. So do whatever will bless you in helping us. Don't mention it to Rosie. She will worry about the money. Between you and me, all right?"

Noah gripped Jakob's arm. "Between you and me. Yes." They walked back into the room.

Noah listened to Rosie's gentle laugh. Even more, he kept staring into her quiet, untroubled eyes. As hard as Jakob had worked to keep the knowledge of her impending death from his wife, she knew. She read the grief in his eyes and felt the acrid taste of a foreign, interior enemy that would soon take her life. She knew.

But she was thrilled to see Noah. As Jakob had said, "She wants to tell you that you made her life happy—and to ask you something important."

Noah's jaw dropped when he learned what she wanted.

Jakob and Rosie were childless. They had loved each other for more than fifty years, but Jakob felt that Rosie had a need he could never touch, a void that only a child could fill. It had frustrated Jakob for decades. But ever since Rosie had rescued Noah from the mugging, she felt as if she had given birth to a child. Her labor had released in her a hope that had been locked away for many decades.

"You are my son," she told him. "The one I never had. I was able to give you life, and this was a great mitzvah *to me. Now I can die in peace."*

She had asked Noah if he were a religious man. Noah told her, then, what had happened to him before the mugging, what had transpired in his heart when he had seen them walking together. He told her about his lack of love for Joan, his lukewarm devotion to Christ, and what had awakened him.

Jakob clearly didn't know what to think of the story, and all the talk about Jesus seemed to alarm him. He folded his arms to keep some distance from the whole thing, although leaned forward so as not to miss a single word or gesture.

The conversation lasted nearly an hour. It ended only because one of the nurses on the floor finally noticed that Noah had stayed well beyond visiting hours reserved only for family members. When the nurse told Noah he had to leave, Jakob stood. "This is Rosie's son. He can stay. He can come and go as he wishes, even if that means I must go, if you find that necessary."

The nurse backed down. Noah stood and said he had to make a few phone calls. He told Rosie he would be back that evening.

Noah and Jakob walked out together. Jakob linked his left arm around Noah's right and placed his right hand on Noah's forearm. The gesture reminded Noah of the first time he had seen Rosie and Jakob.

Never before had Noah felt so empowered to carry out a task. Jakob walked

Noah to the elevator, but neither man spoke until the door opened. Noah looked into the old man's face and felt like a little boy who wanted to hold on to his daddy.

Noah said, "Jakob, there may be nothing any physician can do, but I'm going to find the best doctor in this city to see Rosie soon. I promise." Tears welled in his eyes.

Jakob could not look at Noah. He patted the younger man on the arm and turned away, dabbing at his eyes.

✣

Sam Andrajian was not in his office. Noah found him in the conference room sorting papers.

"Noah," he boomed. "Good to see you. But I wasn't expecting you up here until next—" He stopped, catching the intensity in Noah's face. "There's a problem in Chicago?"

"No, no," Noah assured him. "Everything's fine. But there's something you can help me with if you will. Something personal."

Noah poured out the story, telling Sam everything that had happened since that fateful meeting weeks before. Something deep and indefinable played behind the old man's eyes as he listened—something akin to anguish.

"This Mrs. Harkowitz," he asked, "she saved your life."

"More than that. She—"

"And she's a Holocaust survivor."

"I think so, yes. I don't know the details, but—"

"Doesn't matter. It's all the same story." Sam started to speak, paused, opened his mouth again. "I lost my mother, you know. They shot her in our home."

Noah felt the weight of his sorrow in the room, the grief that had never healed. "I had heard that, sir. I just—"

"It's a terrible thing that people do to each other. But it's good when people help. She helped you. So how can we help her?"

Noah smiled. "I was hoping you'd say that. Do you know any good oncologists?"

✣

Rosie was transferred by ambulance that evening to the care of Mercy Hospital's finest oncologists. She had a private room, round-the-clock nursing care, and a group of physicians who cared for her as they would have served Sam Andrajian's mother. In fact, several thought they were taking care of Sam's mother.

Noah stayed in New York for several more days, spending a few hours in the office and then rushing off to the hospital. Every time he arrived, Rosie would protest the luxurious setting. But like a good son, Noah chastised her and told her that if she kept complaining, he would fill the room with even more flowers.

For hours Noah sat and listened to Rosie talk about her family. It was a new experience for Noah. He had rarely been patient enough before to listen to people tell their stories. Now he listened in fascination as Rosie told about watching her father be dragged away by the SS. She had stayed by her mother's bedside for three days, afraid that her mother would never stop sobbing.

Rosie's voice cracked as she told Noah about the last night she saw her mother. Her father's brother had arranged for the family's escape to Krakow. But the night they were to flee, her mother would not dress or leave the bed. The uncle pled with her mother, even threatened her, but nothing would get her to leave. She would wait for her husband to return or disappear in her grief. There was no moving her.

Rosie never saw her mother again.

"Life is over in an instant," Rosie said, "but the memory of that moment has never left me. I was carried away from my mother, and every other memory of her is framed by the sounds of her muffled cries and her arms twisted over her head. Never have I been able to erase that night. I realized that life is always a heartbeat away from death.

"Knowing that has been my curse and my salvation. I don't want to die. I don't want to leave Jakob. I'm afraid. I would be a fool not to be afraid. But on the other hand, to know that each moment is but an instant from death has given me such a joy in living. I think I knew even when I was only ten years old that people decide whether they will live, really live, or simply go through the motions of life."

She reached to take his hand in her bony one. "You see, Noah, death comes. It stalks. But it does not have the final power to win. So when my Jakob would go off to his store, I knew each time that it might be the last time I saw him. But I never resented my Jakob for leaving. And I never hated my mother for choosing death and leaving me. I simply knew I could not die before my day, and I could not deny that death is ever present."

Noah patted her hand and walked to the window to keep his composure. He knew he was hearing uncommon wisdom. That didn't stop him from feeling desolate.

"Noah," she said to his back, "death is like looking at the horizon on the ocean. You know it is the horizon and it limits what you can see, but you also know that if you could get nearer, you would see further. But the line, that horrible line, will keep you from seeing what is way on the other side. It is like that for me with death. The horizon is all I can see, but I know there is more on the other side. Death has been the one daily reality that makes my life not only small but also grand.

"I'm but a small, small breathing being, and I'm not the Creator. But I'm grateful for each breath I've been granted. Each breath seemed more remarkable to me than any failure or any pain. When my friends would complain or when they remarked behind my back about being barren, I always thought, but I am alive. I am alive, and I will die. My death may be in a moment, so I will hold this moment lightly.

"How grand, Noah, to be alive. And to know I have a son—a son I was not granted until my womb was dried up. It is true what you have told me, Noah—about your Messiah, your Jesus—a resurrection, a coming to life only because death appears to have won. I have a son, Noah, a son. So I know resurrection too, and death does not seem so cruel. I thank you that you were sent so that I could die with my heart so full."

Noah felt his eyes widen. He could not save her, but he wanted to remember her, to open his heart fully to the gift that she was. As he left her room that night and made his way to the elevator banks, her face lingered in his heart like a full moon in the dark woods. His pain was too deep for tears, his hope too great for words.

It was time to go home.

The Idol: "I Will Have a Long Life If I Take Care of My Body"

If you have ever walked into a hospital room to see a loved one dying, then you understand Noah's agony and helplessness. Noah has the power to change Rosie's hospital and physicians, but he can't keep mortality at bay. He can't hold back the tide of aging, decay and death.

The Teacher has led us on a frustrating journey. He has taken a long, hard look at life under the sun. He has looked for significance in a number of places—in control, relationships, work, pleasure, wisdom and spirituality— and come up with a depressing conclusion: *It's all meaningless*. But each time he has gone a bit further and spoken of a joy that can be found in life itself:

> So I decided there is nothing better than to enjoy food and drink and to find satisfaction in work. (2:24)

> So I saw that there is nothing better for people than to be happy in their work. (3:22)

> So I recommend having fun, because there is nothing better for people in this world than to eat, drink, and enjoy life. That way they will experience some happiness along with all the hard work God gives them. (8:15)

> Young people, it's wonderful to be young! Enjoy every minute of it. Do everything you want to do; take it all in. But remember that you must give an account to God for everything you do. So refuse to worry, and keep your body healthy. (11:9-10)

Carpe diem! Seize the day! The Latin phrase and its English translation capture the Teacher's sentiment in these verses. If there is no abiding meaning to our existence, perhaps we should simply repress the question and grab whatever enjoyment we can out of life today. Why worry about tomorrow? Why concern ourselves with the long-term benefits of our lives—there are none. Better to just live in the moment and embrace whatever satisfaction we can find.

Affirming Life, Fleeing Death

The Teacher's point seems obvious to the point of absurdity. Is it better to be well or sick? Potent or impotent? Agile or arthritic? Young or old? Alive or dead?

Much of our culture echoes the Teacher's attitude, insisting that we need to pursue life, health and vitality and avoid, at all costs, decay, disease and death.

Who graces the covers of our magazines? Those who epitomize the forces of life. They are young and vigorous, tanned and healthy. And inside those magazines are articles urging us to pursue beauty, health and vitality with a vengeance. A survey of recent magazines yields the following revealing titles: "Why Appearance Matters More Than Ever," "Why Sex Heals," "The Life-style Makeover: Take Your Life from Good to Great," "Crash Course: Beautiful, Healthy Nails," "Healthy Eating on the Run."

How can we deny of these things? If life is precious, then surely we must pursue the qualities that make life the best that it can be for as long as we can.

Abundant—but Not Painless

Isn't that the appeal of the gospel, after all—life? One of Jesus' most well-known statements is about life: "For God loved the world so much that he gave his one and only Son, so that everyone who believes in him will not perish but have eternal life" (John 3:16). A similar passage promises that Jesus has come to bring a superabundance to life: "I have come that they may have life, and have it to the full" (John 10:10 NIV).

Life is at the core of the good news, and, as many evangelists point out, we don't have to wait until the afterlife to experience the joy of Jesus. Abundant life is available to us right now. Those of us who took that step through God's grace know it's true. Our lives have been filled with new light. The promise of life lies at the heart of the gospel.

I can see this wonderful cycle repeat itself in my sons' generation. Right now my middle son, Tim, hosts a Bible study for his high school friends. And over the past two years a number of Tim's friends have embraced the good news of Jesus Christ, and it's been fun to see their lives filled with new life and vitality.

I think of Ned in particular. When Ned turned to Jesus, he truly "caught fire." His problems seemed to disappear. He no longer dreaded the day, but woke up with a passion to experience what God had planned for him and to share with others his new faith. He truly felt that the gift of a joy-filled eternal life began the second he asked Jesus into his heart. It seemed to him, as it seemed to many of us at the beginning of our journey of faith, that he would never again have a problem.

As time goes on, of course, he will learn that's not true. Because in the fallen world, the abundant life has never meant a pain-free life.

Some of us heard the gospel presented as a way to rid our lives of all problems and hassles. Some presentations of the gospel go so far as to suggest that the acceptance of Christianity will bring dramatic physical healings and even monetary gains. When Dan and I first conceived of this book, we wanted to name it *The Abundant Life: You Should Have Read the Fine Print!* Though we were wisely advised to drop that title, it captures the point we want to make here. For while the Bible promises us abundant life, it never promises a life without care or suffering. If anything, it teaches that becoming a Christian increases our pain.

Paul is the preeminent interpreter of the pain in a Christian's life, perhaps because he knew it so well (see Ephesians 3:13; 2 Corinthians 12). In any case, Paul reminds us that our faith in Christ does not exempt us from suffering. He invites his brothers and sisters into a community of sufferers. And he not only urges us to expect difficulties in life; he also sees their value for the believer: "We can rejoice, too, when we run into problems and trials, for we know that they help us develop endurance" (Romans 5:3). Indeed, he clearly sees the Christian life as a path of suffering on the way to glory (Romans 8:17).

Death's Intrusion

As a society, we have done an admirable job of promoting life. American culture is upbeat, vibrant and young. We can keep death at bay—but only temporarily, as a whole generation of baby boomers is discovering.

Both Dan and I were born in 1952, near the beginning of the baby-boomer generation. The first boomers, born in 1945, have now passed sixty. We are beginning to realize that we are on the gradual decline to the grave. As a result, though we have repressed the thought for a long time, we are beginning to grapple with the reality of death. And once the baby boomers decide to grapple with something, it becomes a major motif of our society.

The Teacher knew of death's intrusion. He realized that the best a *carpe diem* lifestyle can offer was a temporary distraction from the inescapable fact that we are going to die.

If the Teacher were alive today, he would look at a magazine cover and see beyond the fresh, healthy-looking face to the slow-but-steady process of aging. He would see the encroachment of wrinkles and age spots. He would see the straight back and the flexible joints becoming crooked and painful. Indeed, in perhaps one of the most powerful passages of the book, he paints a vivid picture of the process of aging:

Remember your Creator
    in the days of your youth . . .
before the sun and the light
    and the moon and the stars grow dark,
    and the clouds return after the rain;
when the keepers of the house tremble,
    and the strong men stoop,
    when the grinders cease because they are few,
    and those looking through the windows grow dim;
when the doors to the street are closed
    and the sound of grinding fades;
    when men rise up at the sound of birds,
    but all their songs grow faint;
when men are afraid of heights

and of dangers in the streets;
when the almond tree blossoms
and the grasshopper drags himself along
and desire no longer is stirred.
Then man goes to his eternal home
and mourners go about the streets.
Remember him—before the silver cord is severed,
or the golden bowl is broken . . .
and the dust returns to the ground it came from,
and the spirit returns to God who gave it. (12:1-7 NIV)

These are the last words from the Teacher, and they are not encouraging. The book does not conclude with these statements, however. As we know by now, the second wise man comes on the scene and not only affirms the Teacher's understanding of the world under the sun but also points his son and us, his later readers, to something better, something above the sun. But before we turn to that above-the-sun perspective, we must take a hard look at what the Teacher says.

He harshly reminds us in these verses that we will age and we will die. He uses three different metaphors to express this truth.

The first image is a simple one. It sets the mood for what follows. The Teacher compares growing old to the darkening gloom of a coming storm. Youth is a time of sunlight and warmth; old age a time of damp darkness.

The focus shifts to a house in the second scene, though we can still imagine the rain clouds outside. Four classes of people occupy the house, and they are each languishing. It is clear from the Hebrew words, though this is not carried over into English translations, that there are two groups of women and two groups of men. And then these groups are divided into the aristocrats and the servants of the house. The first group includes the "strong men" and the women of leisure ("those looking through the windows"), both of whom are growing weaker. The same is true for the male servants ("the keepers of the house") and the women who grind the grain.

The picture presented in this verse and the next few is that of a neglected house that grows increasingly dilapidated while life goes on outside as if nothing is happening. That is, while the house is falling apart, the almond tree is blossoming and the grasshopper keeps going its merry way.

The Teacher wants us to think of that house as our own bodies. No matter how well we take care of ourselves, in the end the aging process will catch up with us. Indeed, it has already started!

This is the point of a *San Francisco Chronicle* article titled "A Timetable of the Ravages of Age: How a Man Ages." It is written with a somewhat humorous tone, but the older I get, the less funny it sounds!

There are many gruesome things to be said about a man's body as it creeps past the age of thirty. At thirty he's not a bad specimen. A little plumper than he used to be, a little slower, a little balder, yet smarter than ever. Still, his body has just passed its peak. It has started dying a little every day, losing about one percent of its functional capacity every year.

Cells are disappearing, tissues are stiffening, chemical reactions are slowing down. By age seventy his body temperature will be two degrees lower. He will stand an inch or so shorter and have longer ears. No one understands why.

This article sounds remarkably like the Teacher's description. Note that his description of the house and its inhabitants can be read not only as a metaphor of the body as a decaying house but also as an allegory. The New Living Translation indeed translates it in a way that makes this clear:

> Remember him before your legs—the guards of your house—start to tremble; and before your shoulders—the strong men—stoop. Remember him before your teeth—your few remaining servants—stop grinding; and before your eyes—the women looking through the windows—see dimly. (12:3)

This is not a pretty picture, but it is a true one. The Teacher caps off his final litany of death by describing it as a silver cord that snaps or a golden bowl that breaks. Life is something precious, and that is why these objects are described by expensive metals. At death, however, they are rendered useless.

In this concluding speech the Teacher reiterates that death is the end of everything. But he really doesn't focus so much on death as on as the painful process leading to death. He laments the increasing difficulty we have interacting with the world as our eyesight gets increasingly worse ("those looking through the windows grow dim"—12:3 NIV); our ability to chew and enjoy food diminishes ("the grinders cease because they are few"—12:3 NIV); we have difficulty hearing ("all their songs grow faint"—12:4 NIV); and sexual impotence sets in ("desire no longer is stirred"—12:5 NIV).

Aches and pains lead to debilitating disease and ultimately death, which the Teacher describes as a time when "the dust returns to the ground it came from, and the spirit returns to God who gave it" (v. 7 NIV). Something infinitely sad stirs in this description, which is a reversal of the creation of Adam and Eve as described in Genesis 2:7.

Death: The Ultimate Nemesis

Death obviously throws a long, dark shadow over the Teacher's life. Our mortality is the main reason he can find no meaning in power, relationships, work, pleasure, wisdom or spirituality. He mentions repeatedly that it does not matter what we achieve in those areas—death brings it all to an end.

And the Teacher is far from sure that we have an afterlife to put our hope in. At one point, he indicates that though God is in control, we don't know what will happen to us after we die:

> Even though the actions of godly and wise people are in God's hands, no one knows whether God will show them favor. The same destiny ultimately awaits everyone, whether righteous or wicked, good or bad, ceremonially clean or unclean, religious or irreligious. Good people receive the same treatment as sinners, and people who make promises to God are treated like people who don't. It seems so tragic that everyone under the sun suffers the same fate. (9:1-3)

In another place, he questions whether God treats us any differently from an animal when we die:

> For people and animals share the same fate—both breathe and both must die. So people have no real advantage over the animals. How meaningless! Both go to the same place—they came from dust and they return to dust. For who can prove that the human spirit goes up and the spirit of animals goes down into the earth? (3:19-21)

The Teacher is right that the reality of death throws a shadow on the experience of life. We desire health, strength, vitality, growth, and we may have those things, but deep down we know they are only temporary. The road of life always ends in death, and death is usually reached by the difficult path of pain and decay.

Many of us who are now active and healthy, surrounded by friends and family, will spend our last months or years incapacitated in an impersonal nursing home, cut off from friends and family. How do we think about our life and achievements in the light of that future reality?

The Teacher can only conclude: *It's all meaningless.*

The Horror of Death

The Teacher was absolutely right that death is horrible. It's also unnatural, according to the Bible. All we have to do is go back to the very first chapters of the Bible to learn this lesson.

When Adam and Eve were first created, they knew only life; death was not a part of God's work. But then, in Genesis 3, they sinned. And the result, as they were warned, was death. Human life spans would now have a limit. Paul explains, "When Adam sinned, sin entered the world. Adam's sin brought death, so death spread to everyone, for everyone sinned" (Romans 5:12).

Because we know the sad origin of death, Christians should recognize its horror more clearly than anyone else. But often we don't. We repress our fear of death behind pious-sounding platitudes about all being well and God being in control and death not being the end. The interesting thing is that most of these statements are true. Yet they are powerless until we come to grips—as the Bible does—with the pain and suffering involved in death and dying.

As hard as it might be, take a minute to contemplate your own death. Be bold about it. Imagine slowly slipping out of consciousness. You have a few lucid moments to remember those closest to you. You think of the spouse you are leaving behind. You think of your children and wish you could give them one last bit of advice. You think of unfinished projects, of dreams left unfulfilled.

Think about death now from the other side. Perhaps someone close to you has died recently. Consider the pain of loss, the loneliness of separation. Remember how you enjoyed fellowship with that person, how much you respected and loved him or her.

Most stories that we read have a plot that is like a journey. Death is a sudden interruption of that journey; an abrupt and early final chapter. And though we like to imagine death coming softly and sweetly in the night, research shows that this is often not the case.

A study reported on the public radio show "All Things Considered" noted that 40 percent of us die in severe pain (as reported by surviving friends and relatives). Many of the remaining 60 percent feel no pain only because they are so highly medicated. A large number of people die without relational support; alone without friends or relatives.

We should not paint a rosy-colored picture of death: It truly is horrible. It is only as we look death in the face and describe it for what it is that we can really understand the truth of what the Teacher is saying. And only as we comprehend the horror of death can we even have an inkling of the significance of Christ's death on the cross.

At the same time, it is possible to approach death in a way that affirms life and hope. Rosie is wonderful example of a person who has been both unnerved and humanized by the reality of death. Her life was shattered at an early age by her father's death. Then her mother's choice to "die before she was dead" increased her determination to live well. Her inability to bear children who would carry on her name and her memory added to her sorrow, but did not rob Rosie of her humanity: She continued to hope and dream without bitterness or demand. All her life, she allowed the reality of death to shape a deep and abiding gratitude for the gift of breath and life. She did not view her life as a given. Instead, she humbly embraced even the tragedies of her life as part of the gift.

Yet Rosie has no final hope of resurrection, no ultimate confidence in the One who has proceeded her and returned from the dead to represent the victory over death. As believers in Jesus Christ, we are to have no less an awareness of death than Rosie and no less a grasp of the utter marvel and glory of every breath. But we also have the gospel of Jesus Christ . . . and a far more wonderful hope.

Something New Under the Sun

Death rendered life impotent in the eyes of the Teacher. He looked to the future and saw his own end, which led him to question the meaning of all his life. He looked to the future not with hope, but with the oppressive idea that there would never be anything "new under the sun."

The second wise man, who brings the book to a close, is the authoritative voice of Ecclesiastes. We have already seen how this unnamed sage both affirms the Teacher's outlook and takes us further. He affirms the Teacher's view of life under the sun, life apart from God, but he goes on to instruct his son to "fear God," to look above the sun. And for Christians, of course, an above-the-sun perspective has to include the gospel of Jesus Christ.

A key New Testament passage that aids us in understanding the continuing relevance of Ecclesiastes is Romans 8:18-25:

> Yet what we suffer now is nothing compared to the glory he will reveal to us later. For all creation is waiting eagerly for that future day when God will reveal who his children really are. Against its will, all creation was subjected to God's curse. But with eager hope, the creation looks forward to the day when it will join God's children in glorious freedom from death and decay. For we know that all creation has been groaning as in the pains of childbirth right up to the present time. And we be-

lievers also groan, even though we have the Holy Spirit within us as a foretaste of future glory, for we long for our bodies to be released from sin and suffering. We, too, wait with eager hope for the day when God will give us our full rights as his adopted children, including the new bodies he has promised us. We were given this hope when we were saved. (If we already have something, we don't need to hope for it. But if we look forward to something we don't yet have, we must wait patiently and confidently.)

Paul here describes the world as "subjected to God's curse." He looks around him and sees evil, suffering and injustice. He knows his Old Testament and the pivotal events of Genesis 3, when Adam and Eve took the side of the serpent and caused a breach in their relationship with their true Lord. The result is the curse that has ramifications that reverberate throughout the entire world—under the sun.

Paul would agree, then, with the Teacher that this world is the arena of "death and decay," but his view of the future is completely different. The Teacher looks to the future with cynicism, despair and pessimism, because he assumes all life ends with death. But the apostle looks to the future with eagerness, confidence and patience, insisting that we "wait with eager hope!"

What is the ground of Paul's hope? Jesus Christ. You see, the Teacher was wrong to say "there is nothing new under the sun." From the prophets, he should have known that something new was going to happen in the future and that this some*thing* was really a Some*one*—Jesus, the Messiah.

Reflect for a moment on what Christ did through the prism of the book of Ecclesiastes. Jesus, who is God, submitted himself to the world under the curse of the covenant. Paul describes Christ in Philippians 2:6-8 in this way:

> Though he was God,
> > he did not think of equality with God
> > as something to cling to.
> Instead, he gave up his divine privileges;
> > he took the humble position of a slave

and was born as a human being.
When he appeared in human form,
    he humbled himself in obedience to God
    and died a criminal's death on a cross."

Jesus subjected himself to the under-the-sun realm, and "the world didn't recognize him" (John 1:10). According to Matthew and Luke, Jesus' birth was not a grand welcoming of the long-awaited Messiah to Israel; it took place in an obscure corner of Palestine, in a stable. He achieved some measure of popularity in his three brief years of ministry. But by his last days, the crowds of followers were gone, and even the close circle of his disciples began to desert him.

Jesus went to the cross alone in the world. But it was not until the eleventh hour on the cross that the worst moment came. The suffering was already severe, but it reached a point of true horror at the end when Jesus cried out, "'Eli, Eli, lema sabacthani?' which means, 'My God, my God, why have you abandoned me?'" (Matthew 27:46). At this point, Jesus experienced the effects of the covenant curse "under the sun" in a way that the Teacher had only remotely tasted.

And why? Jesus experienced the curse in order to free us from the curse (Galatians 3:13). He died in order to release us from the ultimate fear of death. His death opened the way for us to experience the "glorious freedom" Paul spoke of in Romans 8—because Jesus' death leads to his resurrection.

The second half of the hymn cited by Paul in Philippians 2 spells this out:

Therefore, God elevated him to the place of highest honor
    and gave him the name above all other names. (Philippians 2:9)

The New Testament tells us that we follow in Jesus footsteps. We will suffer; we will decay; we will die. But because of Jesus, we can add, "We will also rise!" The apostle Paul's great chapter on death, 1 Corinthians 15 concludes with a quote from Hosea celebrating the defeat of death:

Death is swallowed up in victory.

> O death, where is your victory?
>
>   O death, where is your sting? (vv. 54-55)

Does this mean we do not feel the pain of death today? Look at Jesus in the Garden as he contemplated the cross. He looked death in the face and he trembled, even though he knew he was the Son of God.

Yes, we fear death; it is a horror. But we also affirm that it is not the end of the story. We live on—because of Jesus. Glory follows suffering. Life follows death. Resurrection follows crucifixion. In Christ, we have a certain hope.

Enjoy the Moment

We have seen that the Teacher urged the enjoyment of momentary pleasures because he felt that what we experience in this life is all there is. His advice was grab whatever gusto we can get out. We have since observed that the Teacher wrongly restricted his views to "under the sun" and did not embrace the truth that death is not the end of the story. Yet even those of us who hope in Christ can appreciate the fact that we should live life to the fullest in the light of death.

God does give us glimpses of joy in the midst of present trouble, and it would be wrong to deny them. Indeed, it is not wrong for us to seek blessings in the present. And as Christians who know that death is not the end, our honest affirmation—"Yes, we will die"—can serve to intensify whatever joy God grants us in the present.

Since death is not the end, thinking about it does not destroy us. And, indeed, when we have a wonderful moment, the remembrance of growing old and dying intensifies the pleasure.

Perhaps you know someone who has had a brush with death and lived to tell the story. Often, after they recover, such people have a new level of appreciation of the small pleasures of life. But we don't need such a crisis to live in this life-affirming way. We only have to take the Teacher's admonitions to heart and spend a little time meditating on our death, envisioning the moment when our participation in our everyday activities will be no more. Perhaps then we will find an increased sense of happiness not only in the special moments, but even in everyday routines like washing dishes or taking out the garbage.

Once the sting of death is removed by Christ's act of dying and rising, we don't have to fear the process that leads to that end. Though our culture desperately affirms youth and vitality and shuns the aging process, we can take a different view and find new appreciation in the different stages of life. We don't have to think that once we pass the age of thirty, we are "over the hill." We don't have to look with envy on those who are younger than we are.

Every stage has its inevitable burdens and its potential joys. The burdens are always there, since the human condition since the Fall has never been problem free. The joys are there as well, if we have the humility and gratitude to accept and celebrate them.

And thus we come full circle. The Teacher said that life is meaningless in the light of death. Paul, on the contrary, asserts that life is meaningful only in the light of death. The difference is Jesus Christ.

Because of Christ, we know that death is not the end, but the final birth. Death is not the final chapter but the first chapter of a never-ending sequel to our life story. Death leads us from a life of struggle, trouble, hurt and pain to an existence where God will wipe away every tear. We do not know the details of our heavenly existence; we know only that it will be wonderful. We know that injustice will be righted and that bliss will follow pain.

Jesus Christ has won the victory over death, and that turns us into followers who are life-affirming and deeply joyful in the midst of suffering. His victory transforms our lives.

Life Above the Sun

Under the sun, life has a definite and inglorious end. Fear of death propels all our other fears and renders control, relationships, pleasure, wisdom or spirituality meaningless. Why bother if it all ends in the blackness of the grave?

Our above-the-sun perspective gives us the answer. In Christ, death is a defeated enemy. The process of dying is a sign of the Fall and not to be embraced as a friend. Yet we know that death is not the end but rather a new beginning, a beginning of a far better story. Death is the path not to oblivion and forgetfulness, but rather to the bliss of life with God.

An under-the-sun perspective fueled the Teacher's resignation to a life of meaninglessness in which

- control will always slip out of our grasp.
- relationships will always disappoint.
- work will leave us frustrated.
- pleasure is always fleeting.
- wisdom is never an adequate guide.
- spirituality usually gives in to legalism.
- life ends in decay and death.

But the above-the-sun perspective charges all aspects of our earthly life with new and everlasting significance, so that

- control leads to surrender to God's will.
- relationships lead to trust in God's love.
- work leads to laboring for God's kingdom.
- pleasure leads to a hunger for God's coming.
- wisdom leads to a humble curiosity to know God.
- spirituality leads to embracing God's wild heart.
- life leads to a joyous celebration of death and resurrection.

The lesson of Ecclesiastes is that Christ makes the difference. Our lives are far from meaningless, because he infuses our lives with meaning.

Taking a Closer Look

Reread Ecclesiastes 12:1-7.

1. As you read this poetic description of growing old and dying, how do you relate to it? Does it describe your experience of aging? If you are young and healthy, perhaps reflect on the aging process as you observe it with

your parents or someone else who is close to you.

2. What measure of hope does the Teacher have as he utters these words? Where do you find your hope in the face of death?

How Do We Chase After Life?

1. Do you fear death or growing old? Is it wrong to fear death?

2. Is it vain to care about your physical beauty?

3. Do you consider it legitimate to use the fear of death to jar people into considering the claims of Christ?

4. What do you like about your stage of life? What bothers you?

5. What beliefs or experiences give your life meaning?

6. Do you look to the future with hope? Why?

7. What Scripture passages describe the meaning that a relationship to Christ offers us?

CONCLUSION

Finding Abundant Life

🕊

Noah's return to Chicago felt like a homecoming for a long-lost sailor presumed dead. Except that no one knew that he'd been lost or that his return had launched him on a different course of life.

While Noah was eager to tell Joan about his time with Jakob and Rosie, he had difficulty finding the words to explain what his hours with Rosie had been like. Joan listened to the stories, awed that they had touched his heart. She knew without being told that Noah had come home even more changed than he had been after the last New York trip.

Noah spent much time that week preparing for the Bible study. He had called Jack and asked if he could take some time to talk about his trip. "Sure, Noah," Jack replied. "But what happened this time?"

"It was amazing. I've never felt more aware of pain and joy. I shared my life and my faith with Jakob and Rosie. I don't know what they thought, but I walked away from them more human and more aware of God."

Joan learned later that week that Jack and Noah had gone over to Jessie's house after work to talk with her about her job situation. At first Joan thought it was strange that Noah had said nothing. But when Jessie excitedly told her that the men had arranged for her to work in Noah's firm on the condition that she would go back to school to get an accounting degree, Joan understood. Noah probably felt awkward about this new level of involvement with others.

"I don't know what's gotten into him, Joan," Jessie remarked. "He was warm, gracious and, frankly, downright insistent that he would not help me if I was unwilling to go back to school. He was so different, but he was so Noah. He had the school schedule and had already figured out beforehand the financial aid the firm would provide and what I would need to save per month to pay for school over the next three years. I'm telling you—when he gets all fatherly like that, he might as well put on a gray sweater vest and smoke a pipe. What's up with that man?"

Joan replied, "I just don't really know. He is different. I can't explain it, but I tell you, Jessie, I like him too."

No one could quite explain or comprehend what had happened to Noah. Those closest to him didn't really need explanation. And those who didn't know him well simply suspected he was finally taking Prozac.

By the time the Bible study came on Thursday night, everyone was intrigued to hear what Noah had to say.

⌘

The study that week would be at Mimi Crawford's apartment. Mimi was the wildcard of the group. She hid neither her past nor her pain, and she could be sullenly silent or brazen and irritating. Her apartment was small but beautifully decorated. Her skills as a trauma care nurse had earned her enough money to feather her nest with an opulence that hid the dreariness of her life.

Mimi had heard from Marcia that Noah was going to talk about his time in New York. She had heard words about his "coming alive," but she was more curious to see if he was as easy to torment as he used to be. Noah always seemed so proper and prudish, it was fun to bug him. Mimi loved throwing out one or two flagrantly naughty words in his presence just to see him tighten his lips.

The doorbell rang.

She thought to herself, I hope it's not Noah and Joan. Lord, let it be anyone but them.

She opened the door, and Noah said, "Mimi. It's great to finally be at your place."

Joan brushed by Noah and put her arm around Mimi, "Anything I can do to help?"

Mimi did not know whether to yell at them to get out of her place or smile and endure another one of God's jokes in giving her exactly what she had just prayed for him not to do.

"Well, honestly, I forgot to make ice. If you stay here, I'll run out and get some at the convenience store down the block."

"You two chat," said Noah. "I'll go get the ice. Anything else you need?"

Mimi's smile turned slightly sinister. "Yeah, Noah, why don't you look for a black kid, about fourteen, with a red Oklahoma Sooners cap. He'll be loitering near the phone. Ask him if he's got any 'dust.' I may need it to get through this night."

She expected Noah to pale and then say something self-righteous. Instead, he grinned. "Sure will, Mimi. I'll ask him to come to the study tonight so you can share with him what Jesus has done to rescue your lovely heart."

Mimi blanched when he said lovely.

Joan laughed, "Mimi, I agree with Noah. You are lovely." Joan hurried into the kitchen and Mimi, whose face had turned slightly red, stood at the door without words.

Half an hour later, everyone except Mark and Suzi had arrived. Mark had the flu, and Suzi did not want to leave him. The others gathered like children before being sent off on an Easter-egg hunt.

Mimi was the one to say, "Well, welcome to my place. It's not much, but it's home. So, let's get this show on the road. You ready, Noah? I hear you've got religion now." Noah laughed the hardest and longest at that one. He really did find himself liking Mimi. Her brusque exterior could not hide her playful, kind heart.

Noah had picked an oversized, billowy chair. He sat down and nestled into the cushions, shifted, sank deeper, and then began the process all over again. Every eye watched his look of intense consternation and his Elvis-like wiggles. The group exploded in laughter.

Noah looked up, and his serious, intent face broke into a grin. His warmth and the companionship only heightened the pleasure, and they laughed harder. Jessie, who was not one to cut loose, wept. Marcia put her arms around Joan, and they shook together like two bowls of Jell-O.

Jack's eyes caught Noah's, and they stopped laughing. Jack spoke first. "Noah, thank you. Whatever you have to share with us, your laughing with us like this is just more than I thought possible when we began this study."

"Me too. Tell the truth, I feel sort of crazy. I would like to keep laughing for the rest of our time. But I also want to tell you about my time in New York."

The room quieted. The laughter did not so much die as slowly evolve into anticipation.

"I don't quite know how to tell you what I have been through. The last time I came home from New York, I felt overwhelmed by the love you showed me. I was really out of control, I know. This time I feel more out of control. But I'm really alright. I know that's odd, but I'm even okay with that."

Jessie eventually asked, "Noah, first tell us what happened in New York."

He slowly told the story. The room was quiet and full of wonder.

Noah finished telling about Rosie's joy at being part of his rescue and adopting him as her son. The story seemed nearly over, but Noah spoke in almost a whisper. "Those two people love each other and life itself with more depth that I have ever known. I shared with them my faith in Christ. They were quiet and respectful, but it was clear by my story and life that I had little to offer them beyond my gratitude and the fact that Jesus had died for Gentiles and Jews alike."

Jessie jumped in. "Well, what did they say when you talked about Jesus?"

Noah said, "Not much. An hour after I shared with them what they had done to draw me back to Joan and to Jesus, Jakob left the room. Rosie looked at me and whispered, 'I didn't know a goy could be so kind or open to learning from us old Jews. You make me proud to be your mother. And this Jesus, well, I will think about him differently now that I have met you.'"

Marcia sighed. "Noah, thank you. I can't tell you what this evening means to me. When Jack said he wanted to do a study on Ecclesiastes, I thought he was nuts. I've loved the book for years, but I was pretty sure it would complicate our lives. And I know this sounds awful, but I didn't think you'd be open to really having your life messed with by God. I'm sorry. I really need to—no, I want to—ask you to forgive me. I doubted God could get to your heart. What has happened to you? It is really important to me to know what has happened to you."

Noah looked into Marcia's beautiful, cat-green eyes. Joan's hand was on his shoulder. He recalled how he had previously looked at her with lust and shame. But he realized that those feelings were gone. He lowered his head and shrugged.

"I don't know," he said. "I really don't know. I guess if I did, I would have some sense of what happened and how to make it happen again. I guess it would help to read the section at the end of Ecclesiastes first. Let me read it." He picked up his Bible from the arm of the chair and flipped to a marked passage. He read,

> The Teacher was considered wise, and he taught the people everything he knew. He listened carefully to many proverbs, studying them and classifying them. The Teacher sought to find just the right words to express truths clearly. The words of the wise are like cattle prods—painful but helpful. Their collected sayings are like a nail-studded stick with which a shepherd drives the sheep. But, my child, let me give you some further advice: Be careful, for writing books is endless, and much study wears you out. That's the whole story. Here now is my final conclusion: Fear God and obey his commands, for this is everyone's duty. God will judge us for everything we do, including every secret thing, whether good or bad.

Noah looked up from his Bible. "Do you mind if I tell you what I have learned from this book?"

Marcia spoke: "Go ahead."

Noah looked at Joan and said to her, "Joan is the one who needs to teach. She is the one who has won me, suffered for me, and prayed for me like no one else. No human being has loved me more than my wife has."

Joan smiled. "Tell them, Noah, what you've told me this week."

Noah started, "I've owned up to what seems like a contradiction. The Teacher is correct, and so is the one who sums up his writing. "Under the sun" is an unpredictable place, and we almost inevitably turn to some kind of idols to help us manage. But nothing works. And nothing is meant to work. Right now I feel less in control, less normal, than ever. And somehow I am happier than I have ever been."

Mimi laughed, "Yeah, well your new job didn't hurt either."

Noah laughed with her. "You are right. Really. I love what I get to do. But to be honest, it isn't what I thought it was going to be. In fact, my real fun now is really in how to unnerve Jonathan Satterwhite by being respectful and kind. And even at work, the bottom line is still the same: Nothing really works, and it is not meant to."

Mimi was irritated but intrigued. She said, "Noah, I don't understand what you are saying. How does knowing that nothing works make you happy? I mean, it ticks me off. It's a rip-off. Like putting your hard-earned money into a stereo knowing full well it's not going to work, or maybe it will work for an hour or a day, but it's, like, going to frizz out on you and drive you crazier than if you didn't buy it. So why buy the thing if you know it will only frustrate you?"

Jack finally spoke. "That's the cosmic joke. You want something. God gives you a taste of it, then yanks it away. Or, even worse, maybe he lets you enjoy it, but then you realize it's not what you really want."

Joan's head was bobbing slightly as Jack spoke, and she added, "I agree. But is it a joke? Is it a mean trick? Or is it a great gift wrapped up in a cheap-looking newspaper?"

"I think you're right," Noah inserted. "I think what feels like a joke is really God's gift to wake us up. Somehow, once I admitted I was really asleep, I could see that God was lovingly trying to shake me awake. I've finally come to see futility as an incredible gift. That gift may feel that God is being mean, I agree. But it jumps out of the blue and snags you, drags you out of the path of danger in order to offer true life."

He laid down his Bible and leaned forward. "Well, you asked. But that is only the second-most important thing I learned from Ecclesiastes. The first is to fear, and to fear what really is the only thing in the universe to fear—God."

The people in the group sighed. They knew Noah was right. But they really wanted to hear what Noah had to say about the joy he so obviously had begun to enjoy. "Okay, I'll bite," Mimi said. "What are you saying?"

"Well, to me, fear is not like terror, but more like the time I went up in a private plane. I knew at some point the pilot was going to turn the stick over to me. I wanted that moment and dreaded it at the same time. I guess fear is both a hunger for a glimpse of mystery and a terror of what comes—"

Mimi interrupted, "Get to it, Noah. First you say it's not terror, and then you say it's terror. Is this just more Bible gobbledygook?"

"Sort of, I guess," said Noah, "but not really. You see, I knew I couldn't fly the plane alone. But the pilot was there, and he was going to do all that was necessary to get us back down alive. Still, I was definitely going to fly the plane, and our direction would be in my hands. So I felt the terror, or maybe the better word is thrill. Fear to me is the thrill of knowing that God has orchestrated my life to know him, and today or tonight or tomorrow I'm going to turn a corner, and he may be there. Or he might not be. Any moment he might or might not appear. God shows up when and how he wants."

He gave her a crooked smile. "I turned down an alley in broad daylight and got beat up—but God showed up too. I wouldn't have seen it at first, but he was right there in the bleeding, the banging of my head against the wall, in the old lady who showed up to rescue me. God isn't just in the small things. He's right there in everything that happens, big or small. But the way he does it is not under my control.

"And so I'm to fear God and be obedient. But even my obedience will one day be seen for what it really is—either my effort to avoid pain or someone's judgment or my desire to join God in his work. You see, life under the sun doesn't work, but God does. He works not to make life easy but to surprise us and invite us to be in relationship with him."

Mimi was still. She gazed out the window. Joan noticed that her face had softened, though she seemed less comfortable and lonelier than usual. When Mimi finally spoke, it was to no one in particular, or at least to no one in the room, "Is it true? Could it all really be true?"

Then Mimi turned to Noah. "I hate you, Noah. I really, really do. You make me think it just all might be true."

NOTES

p. 105   "Boredom is the younger sibling": Patricia Meyer Spacks, *Boredom: The Literary History of a State of Mind* (Chicago: University of Chicago Press, 1995), p. 130.

p. 126   "a high IQ is no guarantee": Daniel Goleman, *Emotional Intelligence* (New York: Bantam, 1995), pp. 34-36.

p. 128   "includes self-control": Ibid., p. xii.

p. 128   "abilities such as": Ibid., p. 34.

p. 132   "I know now, Lord": C. S. Lewis, *Till We Have Faces* (Grand Rapids: Eerdmans, 1966), p. 308.

About the Authors

Dan B. Allender (M.Div., Westminster Theological Seminary; Ph.D., counseling psychology, Michigan State University) is professor of counseling and president of Mars Hill Graduate School in Seattle, Washington. He taught previously at Grace Theological Seminary and Colorado Christian University. A speaker and writer, his other books include *The Wounded Heart, The Healing Path, How Children Raise Parents, To Be Told* and *Leading with a Limp.*

Tremper Longman III (Ph.D., Yale University) is Robert H. Gundry Professor of Biblical Studies at Westmont College in Santa Barbara, California. He is the author of *How to Read the Psalms, How to Read Proverbs* and *Literary Approaches to Biblical Interpretation,* and coeditor of *A Complete Literary Guide to the Bible.*

Together Dan and Tremper have authored the bestselling book *Bold Love* (NavPress) as well as *Intimate Allies* (Tyndale), *Cry of the Soul* (NavPress), *The Intimate Mystery* and Intimate Marriage Bible Studies (InterVarsity Press)